Peeling Back the Layers

A Story of Trauma, Grace and Triumph

Nashville
Black Pride
2015

Lawayne
10/17/15

Lawayne Childrey

outskirtspress
DENVER, COLORADO

Peeling Back the Layers
A Story of Trauma, Grace and Triumph

Outskirts Press, Inc.
http://www.outskirtspress.com

ISBN: 978-1-4787-4041-4

Outskirts Press and the "OP" logo are trademarks belonging to Outskirts Press, Inc.

PRINTED IN THE UNITED STATES OF AMERICA

*In memory of my best girl,
my mom, Renetta Childrey*

Thanks for always loving and believing in me

TABLE OF CONTENTS

1. FOREWORD I
2. INTRODUCTION.. III
3. IN THE BEGINNING 1
4. LOST INNOCENCE 17
5. FOR BETTER OR WORSE 30
6. ABANDONED 40
7. THE GOOD THE BAD AND THE UGLY.............. 54
8. MEMPHIS BLUES AND ALL THAT JAZZ 65
9. HOME IS WHERE THE HEART IS 76
10. WALKING IN MEMPHIS................................. 98
11. BACK TO BIRMINGHAM 110
12. CAN'T HIDE LOVE...................................... 115
13. LOVE HURTS 120
14. WHAT'S THIS WORD CALLED LOVE? 138
15. WHEN IT HURTS SO BAD 159
16. WHERE DO WE GO FROM HERE? 194
17. GOD WORKS IN MYSTERIOUS WAYS..........213
18. GOD EQUIPS THE CALLED 235
19. THE BEST IS YET TO COME........................ 254

20. JUST LIKE HE SAID HE WOULD 265
21. ACKNOWLEDGEMENTS 287
22. RESOURCE GUIDE 290

FOREWORD

I believe everyone has a story to tell and a lesson to teach. When I became a college instructor and speech coach in 1992, I envisioned a life of sharing knowledge with students, helping them develop confidence and hopefully, having a positive impact on their lives. Little did I understand the effect that students would have on my own life.

One student who has touched my life is Lawayne Childrey. He has taught me the meaning of perseverance, faith and second chances. I met Lawayne in 2002 when he walked into my office in Bethune-Deramus Hall at Jefferson State Community College in Birmingham, Alabama. He had heard Jeff State had a speech team and wanted to know if he could join. With his confidence, warm smile and radio voice, I knew I wanted to work with him.

Lawayne dove into forensics with his trademark enthusiasm and quickly impressed competitors and judges with his creativity and flair for performing. Competitive success seemed to come easily to Lawayne. Little did I realize how difficult his life had been up to this point.

When I started working with him, selecting poetry for performances, I did not know that he was a victim of childhood sexual abuse. When we began traveling in rental vans to tournaments across the Southeast, I had no idea that he had overcome cocaine addiction. And when he won Gold and Silver Awards at our national tournament, I didn't yet know that he had been diagnosed with AIDS a few years earlier.

As I got to know Lawayne, I got to know his story. He often talked about the need to write it all down, to pass it on to others as a way to teach, to inspire, to give hope. I'm excited and proud that his story, *Peeling Back the Layers,* is now being told.

Reaction to Lawayne's life story has been overwhelmingly positive. In the spring of 2014, Lawayne had a scholarship created in his name for a deserving high school student by the Alabama Community College System. A month later, he was presented with Jefferson State Community College's Alumnus of the Year Award. He is currently in demand as a speaker, inspiring many different kinds of audiences with his incredible story.

Everyone has a story to tell, and Lawayne has told his with remarkable honesty and insight. *Peeling Back the Layers* details the life of a man who, by all odds, shouldn't be alive today, much less become a successful journalist and speaker full of hope, gratitude, and faith. I hope that this book inspires you as much as Lawayne has inspired me.

Dr. Janice Ralya
Director of Forensics
Jefferson State Community College
Birmingham, AL

INTRODUCTION

How does a troubled, black, gay youth from the Deep South grow up to become one of the most respected news journalists in the country? Some may say it takes a considerable amount of talent, hard work and determination. But for me, it also included an immense struggle through a deep sea of adversities, including a crack cocaine addiction and an HIV diagnosis.

At the age of 4 I survived a deadly house fire that claimed the life of my 2-year-old cousin. Between kindergarten and second grade, I was repeatedly sexually abused by my stepfather and forced to watch my mother being beaten by the same man.

Despite those traumatic events, as early as third grade I had dreams of becoming a news reporter. But as fate would have it, distractions left me blindsided.

Being the only child of a now single mother, I, like so many,

found myself hanging with the wrong crowd. I began shoplift
ing and engaging in devious behaviors, but unlike so many of
my peers, I never landed in the juvenile justice system.

Throughout high school I excelled in my studies, winning
numerous poetry and oratorical contests. However, I flunked
out of college, ended up in a number of abusive relationships,
and as a young gay black man, was spiritually and emotionally
broken and dying from AIDS.

By the time I turned 30, I was the primary caregiver to my
mother, who had survived lung and brain cancer and was now
suffering from a series of strokes that left her partially paralyzed. I loved her dearly, but the concerns over her health as
well as my own left me in a deep depression. To cope, I turned
to drugs . . . first marijuana, then crack cocaine.

Finally, I convinced myself that the only real solution to
my problems was suicide, but I didn't have the courage to pull
the trigger of a gun or swallow a bottle of sleeping pills. I had
hoped the crack would eventually burst my heart, and then I'd
end up dead.

By the grace of God, that was not the case. At long last, I
decided to rely on the faith that had been instilled in me since
childhood. In quiet desperation, I whispered, "Lord, people
are always talking about 'Try God, he can work it out.' Well, if
you can do all they say you can do, please come to my rescue
now."

Life as I had known it changed that day. I checked myself
into an intensive drug and emotional rehabilitation facility.
After months of therapy, I emerged as a new man determined
to fulfill my true purpose in life, which is to speak God's Word.
Not as a preacher speaks to a congregation from the pulpit,
but as a man who humbly tells the stories of how his own broken life was restored, renewed and redeemed by faith.

At the age of 40 I went back to college and became a member of Phi Theta Kappa Honor Society. I also won numerous forensic speech contests and graduated magna cum laude with a degree in broadcast journalism.

Since that time, I've had the privilege of reporting for Mississippi Public Broadcasting, a statewide affiliate of National Public Radio. Industry leaders have honored me with more than a dozen Associated Press Awards and three Edward R. Murrow Awards for Journalistic Excellence. I only mention those accolades as proof that regardless of how hopeless things may seem, if you believe in the Lord and trust in yourself, you can still achieve your dreams.

God placed it in my spirit years ago to tell the story of how he restored this broken vessel, making me whole again. But it wasn't until now that he appointed me to tell it.

As I share my story, my journey, my truth, it is by no way meant to glorify myself in any form or fashion. Instead, it is my sincere prayer that God will use it as a beacon of hope for men and women carrying burdens that seem too heavy to bear.

Peeling Back the Layers is my epic journey of courage, grace and triumph. It is a true account of events that occurred in my life as I remember them. It also demonstrates how unaddressed childhood trauma plagued me even into adulthood. Some of the names have been changed to protect the innocent. It is my sincere desire that this story will serve as a testament to what prayer, faith and determination can do.

"He that has ears to hear, let him hear."

Mark 4:9

ONE

IN THE BEGINNING

I WAS BORN the day before Halloween in 1962 to a 16-year-old single mother named Renetta. If I was the superstitious type, I might say being born on that day was somewhat of an omen for the path that was to lie ahead. My mother and I lived with her parents, James Sylvester and Mary Emma Childrey. They owned a two-story house in a north Birmingham community called Byers Hill. The Childreys had lived up on that hill for nearly 4 decades after moving from Pike County in south Alabama.

Mom was the middle of three girls, Yvonne, the youngest, and Bonnie Jean, the oldest. Aunt Jean had a twin brother named James who was more affectionately known as Sonny. By the time I was born, Uncle Sonny had already served at least 2 of his 27-year career in the U.S. Air Force.

After living on this earth for more than half a century,

some of my most cherished memories are still of my grandma. She was a petite, light-skinned woman with long, coarse hair who loved cooking, especially baking. Nearly every day I would smell the aroma of freshly baked biscuits, cakes and breads. That fresh aroma floated from my grandmother's oven, throughout her kitchen and inevitably filled the whole house with the softest hint of sweetness.

I can still see Grandma in her brightly colored housedresses. She owned several, all in bold colors like pink, yellow and turquoise. They were the kind that snapped up the front with pleated shoulders and a rounded neckline. Grandma used her nimble fingers to make each one special. She embroidered them all with brilliantly colored flowers and butterflies. It reminded me of the exquisite artwork she crafted on the dozens of quilts she'd made for people over the years.

Most mornings you could find me standing at Grandma's hemline, looking up as she stood at the kitchen counter, preparing to bake a cake for one of the neighbors. She'd look down and say, "Are you here to give your grandma a hand?"

Smiling, I'd say, "Yes, ma'am."

Sometimes they were for complete strangers who had tasted Grandma's cakes and were willing to pay good money for her homemade dessert.

While Grandma was reaching up into her white wooden cabinets, pulling out the sugar, flour, vanilla extract or whatever she needed to bake her delicacies, she'd have me rambling underneath pulling out the utensils.

"Baby, look under the counter and get Grandma those two long loaf pans and the big green bowl."

Once Grandma had mixed all of the ingredients and poured the batter into the pans, she'd place them in the oven where they'd slowly bake until they were golden brown.

Before putting everything away she'd reach down, lift my chin with her fingertips and give me a forehead kiss. Then she'd rear back, put her hands on her hips, flash that great big smile and ask, "Baby, are you ready?"

I'd get so excited that I'd jump up and down, clapping my hands and screaming. "Yes! Yes! Yes!"

I knew that meant the time had come for me to lick the batter from the bowl. It always tasted like a little bit of heaven after Grandma had put so much love into it.

Before my granddaddy became a welder, he too was a baker, but not in the same vein as Grandma.

He worked in a downtown bakery where he mixed tons of batter for a variety of breads, cakes and cookies. They would all end up on store shelves across Alabama and many other parts of the country.

Even though he enjoyed his work, his true passion was gardening. When Granddaddy wasn't at the bakery, you could always find him in one of his two gardens at home. The quality of his plants and flowers in their front yard rivaled those seen in the best of botanical gardens anywhere.

Granddaddy stood about 6 feet tall with silver-gray hair and high yellow skin. He dipped Bruton snuff and wore blue denim overalls when he was working in that garden. He'd take gulps of icy cold water from a mason jar and wipe the sweat from his forehead with the back of his rustic hands.

Sometimes Granddaddy would just stand there with his shovel pitched in the soil and his chin resting on the handle. Looking out over his work he'd say, "Ain't that 'bout the prettiest thing you ever did see?"

The front porch was decorated with beautiful furnishings, similar to what might be seen in an outdoor patio or home fashion magazine. There was a wrought iron sofa, love seat and two complementary chairs. A chaise lounge sat catty-cornered on the right side of the porch.

That was the coveted spot everybody wanted whenever we all gathered out on that big wooden porch.

My favorite time was when Grandma and I would sit out there by ourselves on the soft, pillowy cushions, eating her shortbread cookies and sipping freshly squeezed lemonade. We were in our own world doing things we enjoyed, like playing our favorite game.

"Patty cake, patty cake, baker's man. Roll 'em and roll 'em and throw 'em in the pan, for Mommy and me."

It was such a peaceful setting, but what really made it warm and inviting was Granddaddy's handiwork. He set four topiary trees near the back of the porch and hung four luscious ferns from the ceiling overhang. Beautiful evergreens butted against the edge of the steps. An assortment of lavender, pink, purple, yellow and red flowers gave the yard a vibrant burst of color.

Granddaddy's garden was so stunning that it caught the attention of people all over the neighborhood; in fact, all over the city. Folks passing by would often pay him compliments.

"Mr. Childrey, that's some mighty fine work you got there, sir."

Granddaddy would just nod and say, "Why thank you, just part of what God give us to enjoy."

He became so well known for his beautiful landscaping that he started doing lawns for some of the richest white families in Mountain Brook, one of Alabama's most affluent neighborhoods.

While Granddaddy's flower garden was a thing of beauty, so was his vegetable garden that grew in the backyard. An abundance of delicious fruits and vegetables tickled the senses of sight, touch, smell and taste as you entered the gates of Granddaddy's garden. There were rows of sweet yellow corn and patches of dark green collards, blocks of ruby red tomatoes, and bushels of gold, red and emerald green peppers.

He was always giving me a peach, plum, fig or some other fruit to taste saying, "Ain't that good eatin', son?"

"Yes, sir," I'd say smiling. "And it's sweet too."

Thinking back, I can still remember my grandparents sending people boxes of food that we had harvested from their garden. Their bounty helped fill the tables of hundreds of family members, neighbors and friends. Whenever someone, better yet—anyone—was hungry or in need, it was customary for my grandparents to welcome them in and sit them at their table to enjoy a hot home-cooked meal.

My grandparents would say, "It don't make sense for nobody to go hungry with all this God has blessed us with."

Even though I was Mom's only child, my aunts had just as much to do with my upbringing as she did. Aunt Von would regularly read nursery rhymes and other childhood stories to me.

"Once upon a time there was a little boy named L-A-W-A-Y-N-E."

We'd both laugh.

Then she'd tickle my stomach while kissing my face, and we'd laugh some more. Aunt Von would always bring me something back whenever she went shopping. When she walked in from the store, she was usually holding it behind her back. Then she'd smile and poke out her tongue saying, "Guess what I've got." I'd reach for it, but my aunt's shuffle kept my arms and hands from getting it. We'd play that cat-and-mouse game until she'd eventually give in.

"Here is something for my favorite little boy."

It was usually a simple thing like a bouncing ball, a giant lollipop or a coloring book, but it always made me feel special.

One day she surprised me and brought back a box of army men with parachutes on their backs. They looked like the pictures I'd seen of my Uncle Sonny in his air force uniform. I stood there with my eyes and mouth bucked wide open and whispered, "Oh boy."

My aunt burst into laughter, and I couldn't wait to play. I'd toss them into the air, and as they came back down, their parachutes would open up. I'd watch in amazement as they rhythmically glided to the ground. I had hours and hours of fun in my grandparents' front yard, playing with those toy paratroopers.

Early one Saturday afternoon Aunt Von decided to take me shopping with her, but with one condition. She said, "If you promise to be on your best behavior, and I mean, don't be running all around the store touching stuff, then I'll buy you something when we get ready to come back home."

I was determined to be on my p's and q's.

When we got to the North Birmingham shopping district, the streets were bustling with cars and people. There were car horns blowing, brakes squeaking and doors slamming. We would also hear bells ringing as we opened the doors of each shop. After our fifth or sixth store, somehow, I was still holding up my end of the bargain.

Then it happened.

We walked into a five and dime. I spotted a rack with hundreds of colorful silky scarves, and I couldn't take my eyes off of them.

They were threaded through loops and the metal rack could spin around as shoppers looked at the merchandise. Suddenly, my heart started beating fast and curiosity was getting the best of me. I wanted to walk up to that rack and run my hands through every one of those scarves. I was dying to pull one off the rack and throw it up into the air to watch it float back down like my paratroopers. It was as if those scarves were hanging there waiting for me to come over and play.

After a few minutes of hesitation, mixed with determination, I slowly slipped over to that dazzling rack of exotic scarves. And before long, I was turning that rack so fast that the scarves began flying through the air. They looked like kites flying in the wind, and I was having a blast.

By the time the scarves began settling down, Aunt Von was grabbing me by the arm and dragging me away.

"Boy, didn't I tell you not to touch anything? Come on, let's go."

A look of disappointment filled her slender freckled face, and she gave me one of those classic pinches she'd eventually become famous for.

I screamed, "Ouch! That hurt."

"I know it hurt, and there is more where that came from if you do that again," she threatened.

Nearly everyone is familiar with the old African proverb, "It takes a village to raise a child." Well, in my case, there was a lot of truth to that. While Mom was finishing up high school, I spent a lot of time with Aunt Jean. During those days, she was more of a mother figure than my own mom.

Aunt Jean was the one who always made sure I was fed, bathed and clothed. She was also the one who'd take me to most of my doctors' appointments. We were together so much that some folks actually thought I was her son. She still talks about how she loved dressing me up in my little suits and hats just to see my curly locks sticking out from the sides and the back of the cap.

One day when she and I were riding around running errands with Mom, I called Aunt Jean, "Mama."

Mom stepped on the brakes so hard that Aunt Jean had to hold me with all of her might to keep me from flying into the dashboard or through the windshield. Aunt Jean screamed, "Net, what are you doing?"

Once Mom placed the car in park she grabbed me by the shoulders and shouted, "*I am your mama, you hear me? I am your mama! She is your aunt.*" At first it shocked me and Aunt Jean. I cried a little, not because it hurt, but because I was just scared. After Mom calmed down, we headed on home.

Aunt Jean held me close to her bosom and rocked me back and forth. She said, "Lord, have mercy. Net, you could have killed us." But as she thought about it she couldn't help but laugh all the way home. Every time that story was told Mom was laughing too.

My grandparents' house was truly one filled with love. They were always so warmhearted to everyone they met. My mom and aunts often told stories of how my grandparents would let family members from their hometown of Pike County come and stay with them.

"Net, do you remember when Aunt Sue and Aunt Ruth 'nem came to live with us?"

"Girl, you know I remember that," Mom would say. "We had so much fun playing with Bubba, Nellie and all of their other kids. Jean, yes, I even remember when Daddy's brother, Uncle John, stayed with us."

"Oh, girl, yeah, I remember when he opened up that barber and beauty shop in our basement," Aunt Jean added.

"Folks would be coming from everywhere to get their hair done." And they'd laugh saying, "All those folks from down in the country would come stay with us when they wanted to move to Birmingham."

Mom chimed in, "Girl, they thought Birmingham was the big city."

My grandmother's mother as well as my grandfather's mother spent their last days in that old house.

As I was reviewing what I wanted to say in this book, I reached out to Aunt Jean to get an idea of just how many people had actually stayed with them on Byers Hill. All she could do was shake her head and say, "Lord have mercy, too many to count."

When I reached the momentous milestone known as the terrible twos, Aunt Jean gave birth to her first child. His name was Terry.

And just like I had been her baby, little Terry was mine. I looked after him, sang to him, played with him and guarded him with all my might. I was his protector, and as we grew we became best friends.

Now instead of just one grandchild, Grandma and Granddaddy were proud grandparents of two. Everybody says we were both good kids, hanging together like two peas in a pod. But I'm sure we also must have been a handful.

Grandma said she wanted to adopt me and Terry, but with her health failing she didn't have the strength to keep up with two rambunctious toddlers.

Things were quickly changing in that old house. Mom and Aunt Von both got married and moved to different parts of town. Right after that, we found out Grandma was diagnosed with terminal breast cancer. She had kept it a secret for months, but one day Aunt Jean noticed her cutting up little squares of cloth, placing them under her armpit to cover up the sore.

I can still remember standing tiptoe at the foot of Grandma's bed as my mom and aunts held her hands and wiped the sweat from her face. The cancer had gotten so bad that the doctors said the only possible way to save her was to perform a radical surgery, but Grandma chose not to have it done.

"I have fought a good fight, and I'm ready to go home to be with the Lord," she said.

My grandmother died September 30, 1966. That was exactly 1 month before my fourth birthday. So many people came out to support our family that cars filled every street in the neighborhood.

Aunt Jean says on the day of Grandma's funeral, the church was filled to capacity. Hundreds of preachers, missionaries, family, friends and other well-wishers packed the balcony, basement and grounds of the church. They wanted to say their good-byes to the woman who had given so much of herself to help others. With Grandma gone, things would never be the same up on Byers Hill.

By the time I turned 4 and Terry 2, I was still spending most of my time at that big old house. We loved to watch Granddaddy stir the embers in the potbellied stove that sat against a wall in the living room. We would watch Granddaddy put that long stick into that old cast-iron stove and turn those coals until they burned bright red and orange. The flames would skip and dance so high until it looked like they were gonna jump right onto the living-room floor.

One cold winter day after Granddaddy had stirred the flames and gotten the house all nice and warm, he went into his bedroom which was adjacent to the living room. He always left the door open. That way, he could still feel the warmth of the burning hot flames, hear the crackling timbers and keep an eye on his boys.

This particular afternoon, Aunt Jean had gone shopping and Granddaddy was watching us. But after a few rounds of horseplay he became winded and went and sat in his big old reclining chair. As he sat there relaxing he started singing his favorite hymn.

"Amazing grace, how sweet the sound that saved a wretch like me. I once was lost but now I'm found, was blind but now I see."

After a few minutes all Terry and I heard was snoring, *"Zzzzz,"* real snoring. The kind of snoring that you only hear when a man is in a deep, deep coma like sleep.

At that point, I don't remember what came next. Terry or I, or maybe both of us, decided we wanted to see more of those flickering flames dancing in that old potbellied stove. We took turns poking the logs and the coals with the iron stick, amazed at how it made that old burner make music.

"Pop, pop, crack, crack, swoosh, swoosh."

We poked, and we prodded until we had the brave idea to make our own Tiki lanterns like we had seen in the Tarzan movies on TV. So we found sticks and clothes hangers, tied rags to them and stuck them in that potbellied stove.

Before long, our lanterns were burning brightly, and we pulled them out of the stove to get a closer look at the pretty fire that we now held in our hands. When we pulled them from the belly of the beast, at first, they were tame.

We marched around the house with them pointed high above our heads, using them as lanterns to light our way like we had seen on TV to light the jungle night.

Suddenly, the pretty fire began to grow, and as it grew, it fell. I remember when it fell onto the tattered cotton rug, the floor burst into flames.

That's when Terry and I tried to put it out with glasses of

water. But each time we came back with another glass the fire had grown bigger. In what seemed like no time at all, it had caught onto the curtains, and to the covers in the front bedroom.

The whole room was suddenly on fire.

Terry and I were so afraid. I remember him being drawn to the fire like a moth to a flame. He wanted to go into the room that was now starting to become totally engulfed in flames.

All I could do was scream and try to pull him out.

"Terry, no! Terry, no, you're gonna get hurt in there!"

"Granddaddy, help!"

With all my might I pulled. It seemed the more I pulled, the more determined he was to go into the bedroom where the flames roared.

"Terry, no!"

I could feel the heat as the flames started to lick at us and as the room got hotter and hotter, we were both drenched in sweat.

Terry slipped from my hands and ran into the room where he tried to hide under the bed from the fire.

"Nooooo!"

As I watched the flames engulf my playmate, my best friend, my cousin, my screams turned to silence and my body grew cold and stiff. While he lay there burning I stood frozen in a state of shock and disbelief.

The next thing I recall was a man bursting through the living-room door. He was walking by and had seen the smoke and flames billowing from the rooftop. He found me standing in a corner, crying and in shock from the nightmare I was witnessing. The man who turned out to be a utility worker checking power lines along the street saved me, but he could not save my cousin, Terry.

From the other end of the hall, Granddaddy was trying to get to us too, but the raging flames and billows of smoke kept him away and forced him to jump from a second-story window. Even though it cost him several cuts, broken bones and knocked-out teeth, thank God he survived that dreadful jump. Although I never heard him say it, I'm sure losing his grandchild to a brutal and senseless fire must have forced a pain so deep inside of him that most people couldn't stand it.

As the horrific tragedy continued to unfold, Aunt Jean was finishing up a day of shopping. And even though time has a way of healing all wounds, it's still a subject that she seldom talks about.

That's why when I began telling this story I was reluctant to ask my dear aunt to recount her most poignant memories of that day. To my surprise, she boldly shared with me something that I had only heard bits and pieces of maybe once or twice in my entire life. While the story has always been heart wrenching, this time, it was even more difficult to swallow.

My aunt began by telling me that after a long day of paying bills, shopping and running other errands, she was finally heading to pick up a few items from the grocery store. Then she said that out of the blue, something deep within told her to just go on home.

After hailing a taxi, the driver quickly loaded her bags into the car as she nestled herself in for a relaxing ride home. Without any warning, compassion or sensitivity, Aunt Jean said he uttered words in a deep Southern drawl that she never dreamed would fall upon her ears.

"You know they say a couple of houses burned down up on Byers Hill today."

In a voice of deep concern, Aunt Jean said she quickly told the man, "Oh no, I hadn't heard that."

Just as she was about to ask him what happened, he went on to tell her. "Yeah, and they say they had to pull your nephew out."

She said at that very moment her heart started beating almost faster than the speed of sound and all she could do was scream.

"WHAT?!"

Before she could even digest what had just been said the man continued.

"They say they couldn't get your baby though."

At that point my aunt said she was clinching the door with her face pressed against the window as she cried and shook uncontrollably in the backseat of the taxi. It must have seemed as if her whole world had stopped spinning. But through all that pain and agony she said she could still hear the man going on like he was reading from the newspaper.

"Yep, they say yo' daddy had to jump out the second-story window."

I can only imagine how long and difficult that 5-mile ride from North Birmingham to Byers Hill must have been for my aunt.

Surely those few blocks which would have normally taken only about 10 minutes to drive must have seemed like at least an hour. Aunt Jean said during the ride her soul began to sink with despair and she continued to sob in her body and her spirit.

Once the driver reached Byers Hill, he continued the journey up their street to the remnants of the charred house. They passed a number of red and blue flashing lights from the ambulance and police cars lining the roadway.

During the entire drive, Aunt Jean said it felt as if a slow bullet had pierced her already sunken heart, leaving her broken and filled with sorrow. They continued on, past the winding hoses attached to the firemen's big red trucks. And past the crowds of people that had gathered to see the ruins of what was once a place of respite.

When the car finally reached the site where the house had stood for generations, family and friends surrounded the car to help Aunt Jean out of the taxi. After moments of hugs filled with weeping and tears, along with an explanation of what caused the catastrophe, Aunt Jean said she envisioned a lifetime of silence.

After taking several deep breaths, she said she insisted on going into the house where she had been told Terry was killed. My aunt said if she had not gone in she may not have ever been able to come to grips with her baby's death.

With the loving arms of her family lifting her up, she took those steps through the darkened ashes and blackened soot, past the fire-parched walls and water-soaked floors. And finally into the room where she saw patches of her baby's skin melted onto the bed.

Even to this day Aunt Jean says had it not been for the grace of God, she never would have been able to accept the loss of her beloved Terry.

After hearing my aunt recount her memories of that day I was reminded of what the Bible says in Romans 8:38.

"For I am persuaded that neither death nor life, nor angels nor principalities nor powers, nor things present nor things to come, nor height nor depth, nor any other created thing, shall be able to separate us from the love of God which is in Christ Jesus our Lord."

I believe that now, but on that terrible day, I knew I had done something wrong, something horrible. I was terrified. At just 4 years old I had come to know guilt, and I suppose, depression, anxiety and all of the other psychotic ailments that would eventually manifest themselves in a number of ways throughout my life. No one was making me feel responsible for what had happened to Terry. All I ever received from my family regarding that horrific day was love. They assured me that Terry's death was not my fault but rather an accident. To this day, they have continued to love me just the same without any repercussion.

Over the years that followed, I often thought about what happened, but I blocked out a lot. I can never relive the pain that I was actually feeling at the time. I can't really remember the intense heat from the fire or smell the stench of the burning wood or even my cousin's burning body. I can't remember the sound of the man bursting through the door. I cannot even remember the sound of my granddaddy calling out to us.

"Terry, Wayne, oh my God."

Now as I think back, I'm sure my grandfather must have fought hard to make it through the choking, thick black smoke and blistering flames to save his first two grandchildren. Even though I know he was forced to break through the second floor window, falling on broken glass and hitting the ground with a loud thud, to this day, it mostly remains blocked from my memory.

As I said earlier, I've thought about that day many times throughout my life. But it wasn't until I sat down to write this book that I allowed myself to remember and feel the deep pain. And for the first time ever, those memories came with a fresh set of tears.

TWO

LOST INNOCENCE

AFTER THE FIRE destroyed Granddaddy's house, he and Aunt Jean were forced to move into a small two-bedroom duplex in North Birmingham. It was a neighborhood filled with smokestacks and train tracks. They all stemmed from the iron and steel plants that were the driving force of the city's economic engine.

That's when I went to live with my mom and dad, Dexter Jr., whom everyone called Dex. But I kept creating memories with Aunt Jean and Granddaddy.

One of the things that I loved so much about being with Aunt Jean is that she loved to cook, and I loved to eat. Plus, Granddaddy would always pour me a cup of milk with a hint of coffee whenever he'd pour up his cup of joe, and he loved his joe.

Granddaddy would wake up every morning about five

o'clock, turn on the TV and watch the *Country Boy Eddie Show*. Country Boy Eddie, a local country music celebrity, wore blue jeans, a plaid shirt with white pearl buttons, brown alligator cowboy boots and the biggest cowboy hat I'd ever seen. Throw in his country band, a few jokes, along with news and weather and there you have *The Country Boy Eddie Show*.

It was one show Granddaddy never missed, and I always listened for Country Boy Eddie's famous cowbell that he would ring as he recited a long list of birthday greetings. Like clockwork that's when Granddaddy would step into the kitchen and pour up a pot of water to add to his freshly ground coffee beans. He slowly brewed those first cups of coffee on the left front eye of the gas-burning stove, while he cooked his grits on the right eye.

Before I could smell the intoxicating aroma of those deep dark-roasted coffee beans, I could hear the coffee percolating. The top of the pot would shake like it was going to rock right off the stove. It was as if that coffee wanted to dance its way out of the pot, into our cups and through our lips to soothe our bellies. Before we would take our first bite of food or first sip of coffee Granddaddy would always say a prayer that started and ended with, "Thank you, Lord."

Even though my aunt and Granddaddy were now living in a small two-bedroom duplex, Mom and Dad lived in an even smaller house in a community called Stone Mountain. It was similar to what's called a shotgun house. We could walk straight from the front door to the back door passing through the living room and the kitchen with the bedroom on the side. My room was actually the hallway. Yes, the hallway.

It consisted of a baby bed that I was way too big for, but it was all they could afford, I guess. At some point, Daddy took the railings off, but I still slept in that baby bed until I was at least 6 years old. To this day, I have cousins who still tease me about that baby bed.

My mom and dad were both so young. She says she married him right out of high school, partly because of love and partly because she wanted to get out of her parents' house. Mom stayed home while he worked in a cast-iron pipe factory, leaving home every morning before daybreak.

Mom and I would usually lay in bed until about eight o'clock. Breakfast was mostly milk and cereal, like cornflakes or oatmeal. Other times it was bacon and eggs with toast. I guess it all depended on how far the grocery budget stretched that week.

After breakfast, Mom would do her chores, laundry, dusting and everything in-between.

My routine would start in front of the old black-and-white floor-model TV watching my favorite show, *Captain Kangaroo*. His storytelling and thick mustache mesmerized me. I'd sit there and watch every minute of it.

Nearly every day about midmorning Mom would finish up her chores and we'd start preparing for lunch. While she made the sandwiches, usually light bread with tuna or some type of luncheon meat, I'd go to the store to get something cold to drink. I'll never forget those long, hot, summer days.

The store was down a big old country hill, around a long, winding curve and up another gigantic hill. I can't remember the store owner's name, but he would always have my order ready and waiting by the time I got there. Two bottled Coca-Colas and two bags of salted peanuts.

Before I'd leave he would always give me a cool drink of water. He'd also let me take a few spins with his kids on their merry-go-round that sat in the backyard between their house and the store.

Every day, we'd have a blast pushing each other around and around on that giant wheel. We'd pretend we were sailing through the air, letting the breeze engulf every part of our bodies from our hair to our face to our bellies to our feet. Sometimes we'd go so fast that when I'd open my mouth to let out loud laughs of pleasure, I could feel the wind entering my throat, overtaking my body.

When I finally leaped from that merry-go-round, it felt as if I was flying into space. I'd land on the ground giggling and rolling around in childlike bliss.

As I began my walk back home, I'd brush the dirt off my elbows and knees, listening to the squeak of that old wheel and the laughter of my friends slowly faded away.

By the time I got back to the house, Mom would have our plates laid out on the wooden living-room coffee table. We'd snuggle into the navy-blue corduroy sofa to watch Monty Hall's *Let's Make a Deal.*

The outrageous costumes were great, but what thrilled us most was guessing what was behind curtain number one, two or three. I think that may be when I learned to always go for the big box in life.

Despite all the tragedy we had been through that year, it still turned out to be a warm and wonderful summer with my mother.

She was only 16 years older than I, and she was beautiful. Mom had long, wavy, silky hair that hung down her back. Her big brown eyes complemented her thick lashes. Plus she had full luscious lips and creamy caramel-colored skin.

All the kids on our street loved her because she'd get out in the yard and play ball with us. Or she'd wet us up with the hose pipe as we danced, skipped and jumped under summer's hot sizzling sun. She'd even get out in the dirt and shoot marbles with us every now and then. After all, she was just a big kid herself.

"Batter up, let's play ball!"

Those were phrases we heard every Friday and Saturday night during the spring and summer on Stone Mountain. Baseball was, by far, the community's favorite pastime. Every weekend the whole neighborhood would fill up the bleachers at the local ballpark. And their excitement could be heard for blocks away when their favorite player slammed a home run ball over the fence and into the open field. They'd erupt in cheers as the third-base runner slid across the red dirt and into home plate. It all happened as the ball met the catcher's mitt and the umpire hollered,

"Safe!"

One of the most popular local players was Dexter Junior, and I came to know him well. Dex stood about 6 feet tall, with dark brown skin. He had a crooked nose from where he'd taken a slug from a fast ball during a game years ago. But you couldn't see the dent unless you got really close up on him. From a distance, people might say he looked like Dennis Haysbert, the actor with the rich baritone voice who became famous for his role as the Allstate Insurance man.

Even though some considered Dex as being handsome, he was still rough around the edges. His English was broken, and you'd often hear him using phrases like "Yes, I is." Deep down inside, Dex was just a good ol' country boy. He loved going to stock car races and fishing with his dad and brother. It wasn't out of the ordinary to see them come home with a cooler full of the biggest, prettiest bass and trout I'd ever seen. But I wouldn't touch those shiny fish because their needlelike fins stuck my fingers and made them bleed.

Around my fifth birthday, Mom decided to take a job

working in the cafeteria at Carver Elementary School. That meant she had to get up just as early, if not earlier, than Dad. Fortunately, his parents lived about half a block up the road atop the hill.

Their names were Janie and Dexter Gray Senior, but everybody called them Big Mama and Poppa Gray. They were the perfect grandparents, and they had all of my love and affection. I'm not exactly sure what type of work Poppa Gray had done before he retired, but whatever it was, it paid off well for them. They were a very elegant and well respected family. They had a beautiful home that was perfectly decorated and two fancy cars that always stayed shiny and clean.

Their home was a huge contrast to the small, rat-infested one-bedroom house where we were living just a stone's throw away. The rats were so big we could hear them running through the walls and gnawing on the wooden baseboards. I was always afraid they would soon be gnawing on me.

While Mom and Dad were at work, I would stay with my grandparents. Poppa Gray would often take me and my cousin Kobe fishing or hiking in the woods. Or we'd just sit around the house playing checkers while he told us funny stories all day.

Kobe and I were the same age. We both had curly hair and light brown skin, but I was a little chunkier. He had lived in Baltimore with his mother most of his life, so he talked with a Northern accent.

It sounded sort of funny stacked against the Southern drawl most of the people in the neighborhood had. As we grew up, we became best buddies. He and I would often take off into the woods behind our grandparents' house. Sometimes we'd make it as far down as the creek. We'd always end up throwing dozens of pebbles into the chilly clear water to see who could make the most stones skip along the water's smooth surface. I loved spending time along the banks of that small stream, listening to the sounds the water made as it cascaded off the rocks forming a babbling brook.

As we sat there getting our feet wet we could hear the sounds of the birds singing and the frogs croaking along the water's edge. But nothing was more majestic than staring up into the sky, watching the leaves on the trees wave to the sun as the soft, summer wind blew down on us. It made for one of those moments where somewhere down the road I knew I'd look back and think, "If I could only have that day back."

But there were other days I wish had never happened.

Most of Mom's best days were spent shopping. One afternoon while she was out looking for bargains, I was at home watching a football game or a TV western with Dad. It was part of a ritual that we had embraced many times before. Everything seemed so normal that day.

Dad was stretched out on the sofa wearing blue jeans, black socks and a white T-shirt. I was sitting on the floor with my back leaning against the edge of the sofa. The two table lamps and overhead lights were on in the room, and the TV seemed to be turned up louder than usual.

While sitting on the beige-colored linoleum, I began playing with my pocket car. I'd roll it around the floor, then on the coffee table in between watching TV. After about 30 minutes had passed, Dad asked me to come sit on the sofa with him. I thought perhaps my playing had become too much of a distraction for him to enjoy his show. As I moved to the sofa, he remained in a lounging position. Then slowly he reached out and pulled me closer to him, rubbing my face in the process.

Dad had never touched me that way before, but I guess in my mind it was a touch of endearment. Soon afterward, he gently placed my hand over his penis. Without any words ever being spoken, he unbuckled his belt, unzipped his pants, took out his penis, placed it in my hand and told me to rub it. Because I didn't know any better, I took my little 5-year-old fingers and played with it as if it was a toy.

After a few minutes had passed he tucked it back into his pants and refocused on the TV. I eased back down to the floor and continued playing with my red pocket car. But somehow, even at that tender age, I instinctively knew that I had just lost my innocence. At that moment, I think darkness rooted inside of me. But it would be years before it manifested itself in self-destructive behaviors.

I never told Mom what happened because I thought I had done something wrong. I also thought I wasn't doing whatever it was I was supposed to be doing the right way.

What did I feel? I really don't know. But it didn't feel right. However, I soon found out that what I had done suited Dad just fine, because it started happening more and more.

Ironically, my dad was not the only one who took an interest in me that way. His brother Brandon did too. Brandon was a baseball player and was always nice to me. He'd spend lots of time with me out in the front yard, teaching me how to throw, catch and hit softballs. Even though Brandon was very muscular and built like a man, I'm not sure if he was actually a teenager at that time or indeed a full-grown man.

However, I do remember he lived with Big Mama and Poppa Gray and that he would take me down to the basement of their house at least a couple of times a week. It was dark, damp and musty in there, but Brandon would leave the door cracked so some air could come in. As he stood there with his pants and underwear pulled down around his ankles, I would rub and masturbate his penis. But unlike Dad,

Brandon would kiss me and rub my head while he swerved his body and moaned in delight. He'd do that until he ejaculated all over my hands and it dripped onto the basement's dirt floor.

This went on for months, and I never told a soul.

I didn't know why I was doing it.

I don't know why I never told anyone.

I guess I thought it was wrong.

Why?

I don't know.

Maybe because I knew what I was doing with Dad and Uncle Brandon was the same kind of thing that I could hear Mom and Dad doing late at night or early in the morning.

Looking back at those days, I honestly do not feel like those unsolicited acts of inappropriate contact from Dad and Brandon made me gay. However, I do think they introduced me to sex at an entirely too early age. I often wonder what would have happened if I had opened up and told Mom. I've also wondered if therapy could have spared me from some of the demons that would haunt me because of those sexual encounters that happened so early in my life.

For the longest time I thought I was the only kid this was happening to. And I thought I was bad because of it. I felt if I told anybody, especially Mom, no one would love me.

Then the strangest thing happened. One day while playing outside, Kobe and I made our way to the basement. It was the same basement where Uncle Brandon would take me when he wanted me to masturbate him.

Then slowly and very deliberately, Kobe and I began rubbing on each other the way Dad and Uncle Brandon had me rubbing on them. For months we would have regular meetings in that old basement. Even though Kobe and I never discussed it, through the years I've often wondered if Brandon was doing the same thing to him.

While the neighborhood we lived in was called Stone Mountain, it was actually located in Tarrant, a small suburb just north of Birmingham. It was the type of place where everybody knew everybody. They all went to the same church, shopped at the same stores, borrowed from each other and played baseball together. Everyone knew the personal histories of the families that had lived up on that hill for generations. I wonder if they knew everything. One day while I was in Mrs. Rachel's neighborhood day care a little girl named Sarah stepped up to me. Her hair was braided in two pigtails, and she held a half-eaten peanut butter and jelly sandwich in her hand. As she looked me squarely in my face, rolling her eyes and neck, she said, "Dex ain't yo' real daddy."

Shocked is just one of the many ways to describe how I felt. That was the first time I can remember being so mad at somebody that I wanted to fight.

But I was too shocked to move.

She went on to say, "Yo' mama married him; he just yo' stepdaddy. He ain't yo' real daddy."

I was crushed.

Why was she telling these lies, and who was feeding her this misinformation?

I was totally embarrassed and hurt that she could possibly know something about my family that I didn't even know. When I got home I couldn't wait to tell Mom what she had said.

"Mama, Sarah said Daddy's not my real daddy he's my stepdaddy. She said you just married him, and that's why he's my daddy."

Mom quickly grabbed me in her arms and guided me over

to the sofa. We sat quietly for a minute as she held my head close to her bosom and rubbed her fingers through my hair. After clearing her throat, she kissed me on my forehead.

"Baby, it is true that Dex is not your natural father, but he loves you very much. He loves you so much that he wants you to be his own."

Mom went on to say that she and my real father, Walter Henley, never married. However, she said I was a lot like him and someday I would get to meet him. Even though I was bruised, I was still glad to have my mom and my dad, Dex.

It was 1969 when I entered first grade. Mom would wake me up every morning by sitting on the edge of my bed. She would rub her hand from the crown of my head, down my neck and across my shoulders. Then she would lean over, kiss my face and whisper in my ear.

"Baby, it's time to get ready for school."

I'll always treasure those days watching Mom lay out my clothes and prepare my lunch for school. She'd wrap my sandwich in waxed paper before placing it, along with an apple, a bag of chips and a small thermos of juice, in my yellow school bus lunch box. Once everything was packed up she'd walk me to the corner where I would hop aboard a bus with the rest of the kids and head off to Keytona Elementary School. Integration was still in its early stages and Keytona was a predominately white school. But I felt really comfortable there because lots of my friends were also students there. Many of us were in class together or we would see each other during lunch or recess. Even though we were a part of the first groups of blacks to integrate the school, I never once felt mistreated or shunned because of my color by any of my white classmates or teachers.

In fact, there are a lot of wonderful things that I remember and liked about Keytona. One was the campus itself. As the cars and buses drove onto the grounds, the first thing you could see were three huge flagpoles waving the flags of our nation, our state and our school. The main building was made of rugged brown stones and wooden planks that were painted white. The floors were squeaky clean with a shine so bright it made them look wet.

The lawn was always immaculate with colorful flowers, green shrubbery and dozens of beautiful, bright green pine trees. What I didn't like about Keytona was my first-grade teacher, Mrs. Peoples. She was a tall, slender, light-skinned black woman. Her good looks and sophistication gave her a certain movie-star quality similar to Hollywood actress Diahann Carroll. Mrs. Peoples didn't play when it came to discipline.

She was notorious for lining us up single file, then whipping us one by one for an infraction that one person in the class may have committed. But because none of us would tattle, we would all get our butts or knuckles whipped. She usually used the long red handle of an arts and craft paintbrush to do it. I nearly always ended up at the back of the line because I towered above the rest of the students in the class. That meant I had to stand there squirming as I watched them close their eyes and grit their teeth. They were trying hard not to cry when the wooden handle slammed against their knuckles and butts.

I was never exactly sure how Mrs. Peoples felt about me. Whenever we had visitors in our classroom, whether it was a parent, another teacher or even a school official, she would often single me out.

She'd say, "Childrey, stand up so they can see how tall you are." It was so humiliating to be singled out like that. On the other hand, I was excited when Mrs. Peoples chose me to play the lead role in the class's spring production of *Raindrops Keep Falling on My Head*.

I was the lead singer and dancer in the play. Even though I couldn't sing or dance very well, I was a big hit in the show. To this day, I still can't sing or dance very well. But I must say that one play gave me a well needed boost of confidence.

I also believe that getting up on that stage in front of a room full of strangers gave me the courage to face a number of monsters that would soon come my way.

THREE

FOR BETTER OR WORSE

EVEN THOUGH DEX had played community baseball for a number of years, he didn't have the baseball physique like his brother Brandon. In fact, if you were to place the two side by side, you might say Dex was skinny. He had coarse hands from working in the iron mill 5 days a week where he'd often take on two or three shifts a day. His eyes were dark brown and had a slightly sleepy look. Some people refer to them as bedroom eyes, and Dex knew how to use them.

Dex was a big womanizer, using those eyes to flirt with women. One of his girlfriends was named Savannah. She had been his main squeeze even before he decided to marry my mom. Savannah was maybe 3 or 4 years older than Dex. She had short legs and well-rounded shoulders and hips. She didn't have much of a waistline, and with her 5 foot 4-inch frame, some considered her overall physique to be downright dumpy.

With those big brown eyes, bright smile and dimpled cheeks, Savannah was the epitome of that old adage "cute in the face, thick in the waist." She lived around the corner from us in a quaint little yellow wooden framed house that sat right across from "The Pond." The house sat high up on stilts because whenever a good rain came, that old pond would overflow its banks and flood everything along the street. On pretty days, especially weekends, folks from the neighborhood gathered at that old pond. Some were there to fish, others wanted to swim or just take their boats out for the day on the lazy water. There were always plenty of picnickers, and, of course, those spectators who just wanted to catch up on the latest neighborhood gossip.

You could always find someone hanging around the banks of that pond, lined with dozens of willow trees. Those trees, with their long, dangling, hairy-looking leaves, always gave me an eerie feeling.

Dex even tried to teach Mom how to swim out in those murky waters, but she had always taken to the water like a fish takes to dry land.

Savannah and her six children could sit on their front porch and look out over that old pond. Her kids ranged in age from a few years younger than I to a few years older than I. But that didn't stop Savannah and Dex from seeing each other.

Everyone in the neighborhood knew about their love affair except my mom. By the time she found out, Mom and Dex had just purchased a new home in another part of town called Woodlawn. The area had been predominately white for years but was just starting to integrate. It was a quiet community with a vibrant shopping district, including a full-service grocery store that even housed a pizzeria and a busy delicatessen. They served up everything from fried chicken to roast beef to banana pudding.

All of the lawns were well manicured, the schools were academically sound and the people who lived there were hard working and wanted something out of life. It seemed as if things were making a turn for the better for our family. But I can't help remembering the night when Mom and Dex were coming in from a party and she confronted him about Savannah. It must have been about midnight. I was suddenly awakened by the sound of cursing. While wiping the sleep from my eyes, I sat up in the bed to see where the commotion was coming from.

At first I couldn't recognize the voices, so I got up to go tell my parents what was going on, but they weren't in their room. So I rushed up to the front of the house to peep out the window. I saw their cars parked in the driveway, but I didn't see them. Then the voices became louder and more recognizable. They were the voices of an outraged man and a woman scorned. From the front lawn, to the side of the house I could hear them cutting into each other.

"How could you do this to me? How long have you been sleeping with that bitch?" she screamed.

"Don't worry about that shit," he shouted. "You just worry 'bout what I'm gone do to yo' ass if you don't git the fuck up off of me."

They were really going at it.

At some point Dex slapped my mom so hard that he knocked her to the ground. She was sobbing, whimpering and crying for help, but no one came to her rescue except me. When I got out on the lawn Mom was getting up off the ground, and Dex was scorning me. "Take yo' li'l ass back into the house."

Through the light of the moon, I could see smears of blood and dirt all over my mother's face, hands and clothes.

I remember trying to comfort Mom by rubbing her back,

holding her hand and wiping the tears from her face. At the same time she was trying to comfort me by telling me she was OK and that everything was going to be all right. Over the next several weeks scenes like that were played out repeatedly in our house.

Fortunately, things finally died down, meaning there were fewer fights and arguments, but there was still plenty of tension. About a month later, Dex somehow managed to break his leg.

Savannah's husband, from whom she was separated, or my mom could have done it for all I know. Of course, with a broken leg, Dex couldn't drive. One Monday night about eight o'clock a coworker of his, a nice guy named Mason, came to the house to pick him up.

Mason was actually friends with Dex and Mom. She thought they were going out for drinks or going to talk over a business matter because they both did light carpentry work on the side. But without any warning, Dex started stuffing all of his things, clothes, shoes, toiletries, record albums—everything—into black plastic bags and brown cardboard boxes. All that he couldn't stuff in a box or a bag he just set in the trunk or on the backseat of Mason's white Chevrolet Impala. Mom and I never saw it coming.

Things were happening so fast, but Mom just stood against the dining-room wall with her arms folded and tears streaming down her face. Ironically, it was the same wall that still bore the hole from where Dex had thrown her into just a few days before. That night Dex left my mom and moved in with Savannah.

I sat on the living-room sofa with my elbows on my knees and my face in my hands. Everything around me seemed like a big ball of confusion. It felt like the whole house was spinning.

I was devastated by what was happening and wondering what would become of me and Mom without Dex. That's when I overheard Mason whispering to Mom.

"If I had known this was what Dex had in mind I never would have come over."

I was so angry that night. I wanted to hurt Dex to stop him from hurting Mom. But I thought it would be like the time when I grabbed the baseball bat with every intention of hitting him with it. Instead, he just pushed me to the floor saying, "Get yo' li'l ass back before I get onto you too."

The emotional pain was so great that I promised myself if I grew up to become a man, I'd never do anything to hurt a woman or a child. In fact, I made a vow that I would do everything in my power to always love, honor and protect them.

Of course, the breakup came at the worst possible time for Mom. We had only been living in the new house for a few months. Mom had just started a new job, and even though she was making more money, her savings had quickly dwindled down to the bare bones. She kept working, but the bills continued stacking up. Factor in a growing 8-year-old who was bursting out of his shirts and shoes, plus operating on the appetite of a goat. I'm sure things must have seemed overwhelming for Mom.

She never showed it, but I could see it.

We went for days eating eggs and toast for breakfast and dinner. There were also plenty of days when all we had were greens or beans from Granddaddy's garden with maybe a skillet of corn bread. And yes, there were days when the only thing to eat was canned soup. But through it all, our lights were never cut off, our gas always stayed on, and Mom never missed a house payment. Man, oh man, Mom must have been a genie because some way, somehow, against all odds, we survived.

It was a long hard winter without Dex, but thankfully summer finally rolled back around. I guess by that time Mom's prayers had her searching for something more than a man could give her. She must have needed something that would touch her very soul because that's when we started going back to church. It wasn't the Baptist church we used to attend when we lived on Stone Mountain. This was the Eleventh Avenue Church of God in Christ. As it turns out, Mom's family was raised in the Church of God in Christ. Her mother and aunts were all missionaries and evangelists in the church, and they helped foster the organization in Birmingham.

Eleventh Avenue was right around the corner from our house, but I had never noticed it until we started going there. The first Sunday we went, Mom's sister, Yvonne, went with us, along with her two sons, James Jr. and Edwin.

From the moment we walked into Eleventh Avenue COGIC, it was unlike any church service I'd ever experienced. They had a band with drums, guitars, saxophones, and one heck of an organist named Emmet. He was a practicing dentist, but Buddy, as he was known, was also a studio musician and a real heavyweight on the local music scene.

The musicians at the church were the rhythm and soul behind a choir filled with older children and young adults. Together, they had the place rocking. The service was both energetic and charismatic, and I loved being there. Nothing was more exciting than to see people in the audience throwing up their hands shouting words and phrases like "Hallelujah," "Thank you, Jesus" and "Praise the Lord."

In all honesty, I had never seen people dancing and running around a church speaking in unknown tongues. Some of them even danced so hard they passed out. The mothers of the church would come and throw a sheet of fabric over the women's legs when they fell to the floor. I quickly learned that the sheet was to help keep their modesty intact. Another thing I found odd at Eleventh Avenue was the way the preacher would have someone, usually a woman, read the scripture out loud as he repeated every word. I'm told that practice has been around since the days of slavery when only certain people could read and few people owned Bibles. It's still used in churches today as a way to engage the congregation in the message being presented.

On this particular Sunday, they were baptizing the new converts. The church didn't have an indoor baptismal pool, but they did have one outdoors on the back lawn. When the praise and worship service had finally calmed down, we all marched outside to watch the dozen or so people being baptized. There were children and grownups all wearing white robes and standing in the hot summer heat. Some nervously, others eagerly waiting to get dipped into the cool waters that sparkled from the rays of the sun. The baptismal pool sat above ground so those being baptized had to climb up a ladder and down another to enter the chilly water.

Before the baptismal service began the congregation joined hands and formed a circle around the giant tub that was painted sky blue on the inside. The crowd was singing that old spiritual that many churches still sing today before their baptismal service.

Take me to the water, take me to the water, take me to the water to be baptized.

None but the righteous, none but the righteous, none but the righteous shall see God.

After the song ended, Elder Henderson, the pastor of the church, along with a visiting pastor named Elder Meadows, stepped into those cool waters. And with a loud voice Elder Henderson began to pray.

"Lord, merciful God, you have promised to be the Father of your children. We pray that you will receive these servants as members of your family."

Then as the congregation continued to sing, one by one, the candidates for baptism entered the pool. When they stepped into the water, Elder Henderson laid his hand across their foreheads. And as he and Elder Meadows submerged them into the water, Elder Henderson cried out,

"I baptize you in the name of the Father, and of the Son and of the Holy Ghost."

Most of the adults went into the water quietly. However, many of them came up shouting "Hallelujah" or "Thank you, Jesus" or "Praise the Lord."

They each had their own personal way of letting the world know they'd been cleansed of their sins and reborn of the spirit. As the ceremony came to an end, echoes of praise continued to ring out from the church's lawn.

"Hallelujah!"

"Praise the Lord!"

"Glory to God!"

But through all of the praise and religious pageantry one thing continues to vividly paint my memory—the dozens of women standing out on that lawn, dressed in their finest white dresses with beautiful wide-brimmed hats to shade their faces from the hot sizzling sun.

It seems kind of funny that after all these years something as simple as that would continue to stick out in my mind. But over the years I have learned that hats are an elegant and proud tradition for the women of what's often referred to as the Grand Ole Church of God in Christ.

We all finally made our way back onto the wooden floor of the sanctuary where women in white nurses' dresses and hats began bringing around white metal pans. Each pan had a narrow red stripe painted around the edge. One of the women would place the container on the floor in front of the congregants. Another would fill it with water, and the people would take turns washing each other's feet. The foot washing ceremony is a longstanding ritual practiced along with the baptism.

By the time the pastor had finally gotten up to preach it was well past one o'clock. Yet the congregation remained charismatic and not at all bothered by the time. I'm sure over at Peaceful Baptist, people were long gone and probably already seated at their dinner tables. But at Eleventh Avenue they were just in the midst of the altar call. That day when the pastor began inviting people up for prayer, Mom was one of the first on her feet. I didn't know what was happening. When she arrived at the altar, Elder Henderson uttered prayers over her. He then laid his hand on her head and Mom started to shake violently. She was crying, rocking back and forth and waving her hands. I was so afraid because I had never seen her like that before.

As I stood, with dropped jaw and bucked eyes filled with tears, Aunt Von pulled me close to her and whispered in my ear, "God is relieving her of all of the burdens that have weighed her down for far too long." She added, "Your mom is praising God for how he's kept us all alive in spite of how bad our situations may have gotten."

She also told me Mom was worshiping God not only for what he has done but also for who he is and all that he can do.

We had some great times in that old church. I was eventually baptized at Eleventh Avenue and became a member of the junior choir. I had several friends in that choir and on Thursday evenings we would practice the music of popular gospel artists of the day like Edwin and Walter Hawkins, Dr. Mattie Moss Clark and the O'Neal Twins. On Sundays, we'd have the whole church on its feet, swaying and rocking to the beat.

Mom was also very active in the church. She always said if God ever gave her a song she would sing it everywhere. I'm not saying she ever got that song, but she did help to fill up the choir stand, especially on special occasions like Woman's Day or the pastor's anniversary. She also served as the assistant church secretary. When she delivered the church announcements, she spoke with such grace and distinction that some of the young girls would try to imitate her, and so did I.

FOUR

ABANDONED

"WHEN GOOD IS with you evil is there too."

Even though that may be a simple summation of Romans 7:21, it does ring true.

Mom was a faithful member of the church. She loved the Lord with all her heart, soul and might. But like many Christians, she struggled with many of the ways of the world the church taught against. Because of her addiction to cigarettes, it was difficult to give up her pack-a-day habit. She also kept wearing makeup and pants, something that the Church of God in Christ was adamantly opposed to women doing in the 1970s.

And yes, she'd occasionally still step out with her girlfriends to partake of Birmingham's social scene. One evening, Mom and her best friend Virginia had gone to the Aqua Lounge, which was one of the hottest clubs in town. They were there to hear a jazz musician from Memphis named Herman Green.

Herman was a consummate musician who could play all of the instruments, but he really shined on the flute and saxophone. He had jammed with some of the best musicians in the world. Names like Miles Davis, John Coltrane and Cannonball Adderley filled his résumé. He had also been a member of the NBC orchestra, and he helped form B. B. King's very first band when B. B. moved to Memphis from Indianola, Mississippi. But Herman was more than just a musician; he was also a composer, conductor and arranger.

The first night Mom and Virginia went out to the club was the beginning of many long nights that I would spend at home alone. I can't tell you how many nights I'd toss and turn, get up and stumble through the house, peeping through the curtains to see if any strangers were lurking about. Many nights I spent a whole lot of time raiding the refrigerator and feeling anxious about every squeak and crack I heard in the house.

I spent hours watching old black-and-white movies until the television broadcast day ended about two o'clock in the morning. I felt so alone. Even at the age of 10 I'd find myself crying out, "God, please give me the strength and courage to make it safely through the night." So many nights I found myself crying and praying that Mom was all right and that I could fall asleep.

Mom and Herman instantly hit it off and immediately began dating. But it would be weeks before I'd get to meet him. I guess Mom wanted to make sure this man would be a stable force in her life before she introduced him to her son. The first time I actually met Mr. Herman Green was one Saturday morning about ten o'clock when he brought Mom home. I'd been up since about six doing my regular routine:

eating cereal, watching cartoons and running back and forth to the window looking for Mom to come home. Usually the neighbors were out mowing their lawns. But that day as showers of rain drenched everything in its path a big gold Buick Electra 225 pulled into the driveway. Most people called it a deuce and a quarter. Even in the rain it shined like real gold. The water beaded up as if the car had been waxed and buffed for hours. Although the windshield wipers were on, I couldn't see who was inside. After about 5 minutes the driver's door opened. A black umbrella popped open, and up rose a light-skinned man with a touch of gray in his neatly groomed beard. He closed his door, walked to the passenger side and opened the door for Mom.

When she stepped out I could see that he was slightly taller than Mom who was 5 foot 9. While holding the umbrella in his left hand and wrapping his right arm around my mother's waist they skirted across the lawn, then up the steps landing on the front porch. I could hear them laughing as Herman shook the water off the umbrella, collapsed it and leaned it against the black wrought iron railing that framed the porch. The tip of the umbrella tapped the concrete as he set it there. I could also hear the keys jingling as Mom removed them from her purse to unlock the door.

By the time they were inside I was back on the hardwood floor watching TV. Before Mom could say anything, Herman was flashing a big smile, walking toward me with his arm extended for a handshake.

"Hi, Wayne, I'm Herman. I've heard a lot of good things about you, and I've been waiting to meet you."

I shook his hand and told him, "I'm pleased to meet you too."

He didn't stay long, but before he left he invited us over to his place for dinner.

The rest of the day was a typical one for me and Mom. She cooked breakfast, and I dusted the floors and the furniture. She did laundry, and we went to the grocery store. Things were much better for us now. Mom had gotten a job as an inspector at an outdoor furniture company. She was responsible for making sure all of the seams were in place, all the zippers were in line and that no strings were hanging anywhere.

Mom was a real people person, plus she was very enterprising. Since she was spending so much time at the club with Herman, she decided to take a part-time job there. The club owner said she was the best waitress he had, and it was evident from all the tips she was bringing home.

She'd use a large part of that money to drag me from store to store in search of size 18 husky pants. Sometimes Mom would get so frustrated from having to shop all over town to find pants in that size, she'd say, "Wayne, you have got to lose some weight or we're not going to be able to find you anything, baby."

Thinking back, even at that tender age I was using food to mask much of the pain I had already endured in my young life. Whenever we were lucky enough to find those 18 huskies Mom would usually go ahead and buy them all up. Even if it meant getting the same pair in every color or pattern.

Mom's swag was incredible. I loved seeing her wearing her big Afro wig, giant hoop earrings, halter tops and wide-legged pants. My mom who gave birth to me as a 16-year-old girl had blossomed before my eyes into a beautiful woman, with class, dignity and lots of personal style. Yes, Ms. Renetta had turned out to be quite a woman, and men adored her, especially Herman.

As we drove to his house for dinner I couldn't help but ask my mother, "Is he rich?"

She laughed and asked, "Baby, what makes you think he's rich?"

I told her, "All of the homes around here are so big and all of the cars so fine it looks like he could be rich."

She laughed again and said, "There are a lot of ways to be rich, baby. It's not always about having lots of money. Being rich has more to do with being happy with what you have. Being rich is about having enough. Some people working minimum-wage jobs are rich, while many with millions in the bank may be rich in finances but poor in spirit."

Entering the driveway we passed the huge brick house and drove around to the backyard. There were four cars in paved parking spaces like at the mall. We parked in the fifth and last spot. Before getting out of the car Mom reminded me to be on my best behavior.

"Don't forget to lay your napkin across your lap and use your utensils the way I taught you," she said. "And, oh yeah, please keep your elbows off the table. OK, son?"

I agreed and was anxious to go inside.

When we got out of the car I headed straight to the back door of that big old house. Mom called out, "We're going here."

It was actually a garage with an upstairs apartment. By the time we made it to the top of the stairs Herman was in the doorway welcoming us in.

"Hey, come on in, baby," he said, as he kissed Mom on the lips. "Hey, Wayne, son, come on in and make yourself at home."

Herman's place was so fly or hot or whatever floats your boat, but it was very nice. The whole apartment had a masculine color palate of black and chrome with touches of red. Dramatic, colorful African art paintings and sculptures embraced the walls and tables. One room was totally filled with music and recording equipment in cabinets that ran from the floor to the ceiling. Soft mood lights accentuated everything and the sounds of Miles Davis set the tone for a perfect evening. Even though this was like a scene I had only seen on TV, I knew that one day this would become my kind of style.

The dinner was perfect. The steak was juicy and tender, the salad cool and crisp. And "ahhh" . . . the baked potato stuffed with cheese, sour cream, bacon bits and butter melted in my mouth.

After dinner, Herman went to his bedroom and brought out his beautiful long-haired dachshund named Derry.

Mom freaked out!

She was attacked by a dog when she was growing up on Byers Hill. The only thing that saved Mom then was a car that came by with his lights on and scared the dog away. Since then Mom has been afraid of dogs, even the tiniest of dogs like Derry. But for some odd reason Mom seemed to be a little cozier with this dog than I'd ever seen her with any other.

As with most musicians, all good gigs must come to an end. Herman's time at the Aqua was winding down, and he had another gig lined up in Memphis. By that time he and Mom were dating heavily. He didn't want to go back, and she didn't want him to go.

When Herman started playing at the new club in Memphis, Mom and I would go up to visit him some weekends. Mom and Herman would stay at a hotel. I'd stay at Herman's parents' house.

Everyone called his mom, Mother Green. By the time we met she had suffered a number of strokes that left her partially paralyzed. Mother Green was a tall, light-skinned, strongly opinionated woman. She had a real flair for fashion, but because of her illness, most of the evidence of her personal style was left hanging up in her wardrobe or captured in a photo album. Her husband, Elder Tigner Green, had once been an affluent pastor in the Church of God in Christ which is headquartered in Memphis. He had since relinquished his pastoral duties because of his battle with the early stages of Alzheimer's.

The Greens lived on Texas Street in South Memphis. During its heyday, Texas Street had been home to doctors, lawyers and school principals. Even famous musicians like B. B. King and Aretha Franklin had lived in the area. By the mid-'70s, many of the people on Texas Street had started moving away into other more affluent neighborhoods. Others had retired or, like the Greens, were sickly and couldn't afford the upkeep on their once immaculate homes and lawns.

Like so many black neighborhoods across the country, South Memphis was starting to change but the sense of family remained strong. On the right side of the Greens lived the Moores, a middle-class family of professionals. The matriarch was a retired schoolteacher. Her daughter who was also her caregiver was a high school principal. I got to know her two children, Alanna and Kenton. They were cool, talented and brilliantly gifted students. Kenton was also very athletic. We'd go from playing basketball in the backyard to ping-pong in their driveway. Alanna was just as pretty as Thelma on *Good Times*. She exuded so much talent that we knew she was priming herself for greatness on Broadway, in the boardroom or on Wall Street.

Across the street from the Greens were the Harrisons, another multigenerational family living under one roof. There was Anna, who was extremely obese. She didn't work an official job, but she did stay home to help take care of her elderly and sickly mother. Anna also took care of her four sisters and brothers, one of which was a young petty marijuana dealer. There was a dealer on almost every block.

To the left of the Greens were the Wilsons, an elderly couple with two sons who were at least 20 years apart. One was about 40, but he was a really cool 40-year-old. We all called him Dude. He worked as a supervisor at the post office and drove one of the coolest cars I'd ever seen. It was a 1969 convertible top Cadillac Seville in candy-apple red. It was tricked out with red and white leather seats, chrome accessories and it drove like a whisper. His younger brother, Theo, was just the opposite. He drove a black two-seater muscle car with lots of "*vroom vroom vroom.*" We could always tell when he was coming home because we could hear the beats and feel the vibes of his radio or 8-track tape player a block away.

Just up the block was Mr. Chen's Grocery. It was a typical corner store. Folks could shop for their groceries and pay their bill at the end of the month or when they got paid. It was the type of store where you could get everything from bunches of collard greens, to 50 cents' worth of hoop cheese to a juicy beef roast cut to your specifications. I'd usually end up there at least once a day for a dill pickle or a Nehi soft drink. And sometimes I'd get one of those cookies that he sold out of a big plastic tub on the counter by the cash register. I think the best thing about Chen's was that if you didn't have the money you could put it on your family's charge account.

The eclectic vibe of Texas Street stole my heart. But what I loved about it most was Herman's oldest daughter Andrea, and her daughter Tonya who was about 3 years younger than I. They stayed with Elder and Mother Green. I loved them the first time I met them.

Andrea was young, fashionable and sophisticated. She loved eating out, going to movies, plays and concerts. She even enjoyed taking late-night trips to the store or anywhere just to get out of the house. "Classy" described her to the tee. I was already looking forward to getting back to Memphis to spend more time with them.

Even though I thought Herman was good for my mom, there was something about their relationship that I didn't fully understand.

Why did he have to take so much of her time away from me?

It seemed like every weekend she was driving up to Memphis to be with him, but I started staying behind. It got to the point that when Mom was packing her bag to go to Memphis, I was packing my bag to go stay with my aunts for the weekend. After months of this routine, Mom's sisters became concerned about her spending so much time with a man they barely knew. I think what concerned them most was that they felt I was being neglected and passed around too much. Of course, they didn't mind keeping me. They loved me, and I loved them. We have always been a very close family. However, all they saw was a woman who had suddenly abandoned her family, her church and her friends to be with a jazz musician.

All week long, Mom planned her weekend getaway. She glowed with excitement, bought a couple of new outfits and got her hair and nails done. As she did the dishes she was often singing her favorite Al Green and Barry White love songs. It was obvious she was a woman in love. When she got off work that Friday she rushed home, packed her bags and had me pack mine. She then called Aunt Jean to tell her she was dropping me off. But this time Aunt Jean said no, she couldn't keep me because she had something that she had planned to do.

I heard Mom on the phone debating what my aunt had to

do that was so important that I couldn't even stay there with Granddaddy. I don't know what was said, but her answer was still no.

After their heated conversation, Mom called Aunt Von. I really liked staying with Aunt Von, Uncle James and their kids because they were kind of like the Brady Bunch or some of those other families I'd seen on TV. They were the type that had breakfast, lunch and dinner at the table together. They also took family outings and owned a beautiful home and pretty cars.

But like Aunt Jean, Aunt Von also said no that day. They felt like Mom was going too fast with Herman. My aunts wanted her to refocus on what they thought should take prominence in her life: her son, her family and her faith. After Aunt Von's rejection, Mom turned to her friends, Eva and Virginia, but they were both unavailable.

To make things worse, Andrea and Tonya were in Chicago that weekend. And it would have been awkward to ask Herman's aunt, who was taking care of his ailing parents, to take care of me too.

So what's a mom to do? Postpone her trip to another weekend or leave her 10-year-old son at home by himself?

Mom chose to leave me home alone.

Before she left, she sat me down and told me how much she loved me.

"Baby, you know I want to take you with me, but Herman and I will be going to Little Rock, Arkansas." She said, "Herman is going to be playing a gig for some big-time event with the governor, and there won't be any kids there."

Mom showed me there was food in the fridge. And she made me promise to adhere to a laundry list of things that she didn't want me to do while she was away.

"Don't leave the house."
"Don't go outside."
"Don't answer the phone."
"Don't let anyone know that I'm not home."
"Don't let anyone know you're home alone."

Mom even told me which lights and TV to leave on each night so that everything looked normal. I was scared to death, but I didn't let her see it.

When she left it was already starting to get dark. Even with the TV on, I could still hear every squeak of the house, every chirp of the birds, and every hum of the locust. I could hear my friends outside playing hide-and-seek in the yards all around our house.

"5, 10, 15, 20, 25, 30, 35, 40, 45, 50, 55, 60, 65, 70, 75, 80, 85, 90, 95, 100."

"All not ready holler billy goat."

I guess I finally fell asleep listening to the steady stop-and-go of traffic outside. I'd often slip into Mom's bed when she wasn't home. I guess it just felt better, or maybe it made me feel as if some part of her was there with me.

Suddenly, I woke up to *"SSSHHH,"* that white noise the TV would make back then after the broadcast day had ended. That's all you'd get after they had signed off the air with their stations' rules and regulations, or the video of the American flag flying to the tune of the National Anthem.

It must have been about 2:30 a.m. I remember getting up out of the bed, turning off the TV, tiptoeing to the living room and peeping out of the window. That's when it hit me I was at home by myself, and I would be at home by myself for at least two more nights. A spirit of fear fell upon me.

"What if I get sick or the house catches on fire or someone tries to break in?"

These were all questions running through my mind. I felt all alone and started to wonder if Mom was all right. Then my thoughts turned darker. Would my mom really come back to me or had I been abandoned and left to fend for myself forever?

As tears rolled down my face I prayed to God that I would survive that weekend and that Mom would make it home safely. I also prayed that neither I nor any child would have to be alone again.

When day broke, things were just as scary and eerie as the night had been. I could still hear the house squeaking, the birds singing and the kids outside playing on the sidewalk.

Still I felt alone, afraid and ashamed.

I was afraid somebody would come to the house and find out that Mom had left me at home alone to go out of state to be with her boyfriend. That feeling returned even when Mom was at work late or just away shopping sometimes. But it was during that time that I began writing songs and poems to express everything I was feeling inside. It was like having an imaginary friend to talk to and share all of my secrets with.

As I am writing this book I have to pause and pinch myself because it's almost like being 10 years old again, sitting in my bed, writing my very first song.

Wings of a Dove

If I had the wings of a dove, I'd fly away

Way up in the sky.

And if I had the wings of a dove,

I'd tell this old world good-bye.

I'd get on the runway

Make a quick takeoff.

I'd be so high

But my soul never would be lost.

I'd look all around

To see what I could see

If I entered danger

I know the Lord would rescue me

Sometimes I feel

Like flying away.

Writing became my life.

I could be anywhere, doing anything at any time and suddenly I'd get an inspiration to just write. Sometimes it was sparked by something someone said, sometimes it was what someone did, but whenever the urge hit me I had to write. So I started carrying around a little notepad and pen. Before long I had so many songs and poems written that my notebook was full and I had to get another one.

I thank God for whispering the words in my ear because even to this day it continues to soothe my doubts and calm my fears.

When Mom got back home early Monday morning after that scary weekend, I was so happy to see her. With tears in her eyes, she hugged me and gave me the most sincere apology I've ever heard, and I accepted it without any reservations. It didn't matter anymore that I had been left home alone. I knew my mom didn't mean me any harm. Even then, I understood that it was a gamble she took in hopes of making our lives better.

I never held it against her.

That scenario was never repeated. However, those feelings of abandonment and not wanting to be alone continued to haunt me for years.

FIVE

THE GOOD THE BAD AND THE UGLY

"LAWAYNE CHILDREY BECOMES WBRC TV's First African American News Anchor"

That's the news headline I'd dreamed of for years. In fact, by the time I reached sixth grade I was completely focused on becoming a news reporter. So I would run home after school, change out of my "school clothes" and into my "play clothes." Then I'd fix myself a ham sandwich or whatever was convenient, drown it down with a glass of chocolate milk and do my homework. I wanted to get it out of the way so I'd have plenty of time to head out the door to play with my friends Ernest, Audrey and Tyrone Belser.

The Belsers were a sister-and-brother trio who lived across the street from me. We would do everything together, like playing dodgeball, hide-and-seek, hopscotch or football in the street. We were a pretty normal bunch of kids, but we could be mischievous too. Late one afternoon we were on the Belsers' front porch playing around on their rock and concrete banister. It was the kind that was so wide you could use it to set plants on. They would use it as extra seating when all of the chairs on the porch were taken.

One day Ernest was standing up on the banister practicing his acrobatic balancing act. In the process he inadvertently noticed that he could see over into Ms. Ava's living-room window. Ms. Ava was a spunky woman who had several daughters living with her. And as two normal preteen boys, we noticed.

As Ernest continued to balance himself he caught a brief glimpse of a woman who had shed her blouse and bra. Finally she was rubbing her breasts in a way that reflected someone who was relieved to be free of the contraption. Needless to say we took turns standing up on that banister peeping over into Ms. Ava's window and laughing at her bare breasts. They were so big it looked as if they hung all the way down to her waist. We thought watching Ms. Ava's nakedness was the funniest thing we had ever seen. However, the fun came to a halt when she caught on and draped the window.

But regardless of how much fun we were having watching Ms. Ava, playing dodge ball or hide-and-seek, I would always make it home by 5:30. That was my time to be plopped in front of the TV to watch quintessential newsman Walter Cronkite do the CBS Evening News. I've always had a thing for great voices, and his voice was the ultimate one. I longed to hear him do all 30 minutes of the CBS evening news, including his famous sign-off line.

"And that's the way it is."

That's also the way I got hooked on news. Watching Cronkite also strengthened my desire to someday become an anchor on Channel 6 in Birmingham.

I must have gotten at least part of my love for English, grammar and reading from Mom's family. She and my aunts would sometimes tell my cousins and me about a joke that was going around their neighborhood when they were growing up on Byers Hill. The joke was that the Childrey kids, meaning Mom, along with her two sisters and brother, would go home after school and practice their speech pattern so they could sound proper. That's a term some black Southerners still used to ridicule other blacks for speaking English correctly, or, as they also say, for trying to "sound white."

For the record, the part about practicing their speech may have been true. I'm not saying it was, but it could have been. But I do know that it wasn't to make them sound white. Even though my granddad and his siblings were all listed on their birth certificates as mulatto, they were always proud of our African American heritage. And they always embraced our rich culture and customs.

At Dupuy Elementary School, I had the good fortune of being exposed to a wonderful teacher who noticed my love for reading and speaking at an early age. Mrs. Easley taught sixth-grade English. Her brother had been an integral part of Dr. Martin Luther King Jr.'s inner circle to fight injustice during the civil rights era. Mrs. Easley would often have me on school assembly programs extending the welcome, reciting a poem or presenting a speaker to our students. Just as my first-grade teacher, Mrs. Peoples, would often ask me to stand up in front of visitors to show them how tall I was, Mrs. Easley would do something similar.

She would have me to stand up and show visitors how well I could read. It was usually a poem or some passage from a book. One day, Mrs. Easley called me and about 10 other students into the library. We had been chosen to participate in a special program sponsored by the Alabama Department of Education.

The goal was to have students write and produce a radio-type soap opera that dealt with issues that were affecting children in a negative way. We came up with a court show where the parents had been accused of abusing their kids. Each of us played a different role. There was a mother, father, abused child, social worker, attorneys, a judge and witnesses. I played the judge, but we all participated in developing the plot, writing the script and developing the characters.

Once we had everything in order we were taken to the Alabama Public Radio studios. They were housed in Phillips High School, one of the oldest high schools in Birmingham. The building was made of huge brownstones and from my child's-eye view, it resembled a castle. We were all placed in a small room with walls that were padded in a foam-type covering. The floor was carpeted, and each one of us had a microphone, along with headphones, that allowed us to hear ourselves as we spoke. Black metal stands were placed in front of us.

They were similar to what musicians use to hold their sheets of music, but in our case, they were holding our scripts. The room was cold and dark with only a spotlight shining down on each music stand. The oversized glass window gave us a direct view of the director and sound engineer as they sat in front of the giant mixing board. The control booth was impressive. It was filled with buttons that they used to adjust the volume as we spoke and others let them add sound effects like doors opening, the judge banging his gavel and chairs sliding back and forth from the defendant's table. The engineer also plugged in the sounds of footsteps as witnesses made their way across the wooden floor up to the witness stand where the gate squeaked as they pushed it open. As the person sat down to testify you could again hear the chair scraping as they adjusted in their seat.

The finished product sounded amazing. It was the first time I had ever helped produce a show, done voice-over work or heard myself on tape, and it felt wonderful. The recording eventually made its way into libraries and classrooms all over Alabama. Hopefully, it served its purpose, which was to bring awareness to the growing problem of child abuse and ways to detect and report it.

As long as I was in school I remained focused on things that were important. The routine gave much-needed structure to my life. But when summer came around, I was home alone and ended up way over my head. During those long summer days, my friends and I would visit each other's houses while our parents were at work. It was something I was told explicitly not to do, but with Mom at work all day, I didn't think she'd ever know.

Audrey, Ernest, Tyrone and I, along with the Carson kids and a few more people, would gather at each other's houses to have little parties. We'd listen to music on the radio or our parents' vinyl collection on their record players. Yes, indeed, we'd be jamming to some Ohio Players, The Jackson 5, The O'Jays, all those now old-school greats.

At 10, 11 and 12 years old, we were way too young to be into the drinking or drugging scene, but we did love to party. And what is a great party without great food? We weren't rich, but we always found something. We'd rumble through our parents' kitchen and pull out snacks like popcorn, potato chips and soft drinks. We were cool with that menu, but there was a guy who lived down the street who thought we could do a little better.

Larry was the one person that our parents forbade us from hanging with because he was the epitome of trouble. He was always getting into undesirable situations at school and he had a reputation for being a bully. Plus, he was a slow walker who always wore caps and baggy layers of clothes, even in the summertime.

The day he came to one of our parties bearing gifts of chocolates, drinks and cookies, Ernest asked him, "Where you get all this food?"

Larry said, "I stole it from the grocery store up on Tenth Avenue."

We were all intrigued by his cunning abilities. He constantly solicited us to join him in his endeavors playing tricks on the neighborhood, and he succeeded, but I got caught. Larry did his dirty work early in the mornings. So the next day he waited until my mom had pulled out of the driveway on her way to work before he came and rang our doorbell. As soon as he came into the house he gave me a crash lesson on how to steal.

"Walk into the store and go directly to what you want to get," he said. "Then lift up your shirt, stick the stuff in your pants and pull your shirt back down." He continued, "Just walk right out like you didn't find what you were looking for."

As Larry and I began to make our way up to Dixie Supermarket, my stomach was boiling with anxiety. It was so early in the morning that the dew was still on the grass and the street was quiet because all of my friends were still asleep. The store was about three blocks from my house, and with every step I felt like I had made a deal with the devil that I couldn't take back. Even at that age, I had become a people pleaser. I thought if I changed my mind Larry would think I was a coward and wouldn't like me or be my friend anymore, so I kept up a strong front.

When we got to Dixie there were only a handful of people shopping and the short row of checkout lines were empty. I made my way to the candy aisle and scanned the shelves for the big bags of Hershey's kisses. Quickly lifting my T-shirt like Larry had told me, I placed a bag of the chocolates in my pants. Sweat was popping off my forehead and running down my neck as nerves got the best of me. The crinkled plastic bag made much more noise that I had bargained for.

I felt like I was an obvious target.

So I looked around to see if anybody was looking before I stuffed another bag into my pants. That's when I headed toward the door. But as I arrived near the register I saw Larry sitting in the office that sat high up on a platform near the store entrance.

The manager was a short Italian man with curly silver-gray hair and a hump in his back. He had caught Larry stuffing bags of peanuts down his pants. As I approached the door the manager told me to take the chocolates out that I had stuffed in my pants. Sweat was pouring down my face and dripping from the tip of my nose. My knees started shaking, and I felt sick in my stomach, like I wanted to throw up.

The man was obviously upset as he ranted at Larry. "I knew you were full of games," he said. "I've been watching you for weeks."

But when he started talking to me, he stopped in his tracks and looked me directly in my eyes with a look of compassion.

"Son, I don't want you to end up following in this young man's footsteps because I know you're really a good kid with lots of potential. But I'm going to have to teach you boys a lesson that I hope will stick with you. That's why I'm calling the police to take your butts to juvenile hall."

Before the police arrived, a woman who lived on the same street as Aunt Von came into the store. Sister Crenshaw was her name. I remember that because she was also a member of our church, and they always addressed the women as sister this or sister that.

She spotted me sitting up in the office when she entered the store. So she asked the manager what was going on. Of course he told her that we were getting into big trouble and that he was waiting for the police to pick us up. I'm not sure if she even finished her shopping before she went and told my aunt what had happened.

When the police finally came I remember feeling cheap and humiliated as many of the neighbors saw me and Larry getting into the police car. Needless to say, I was scared. All kinds of questions were going through my mind.

How long will I be in jail? What are they going to do to me? Is Mom gonna beat my butt?

It seemed to take forever to get across town to the juvenile detention center. The whole time I was sitting in the back of that police car I couldn't help but think how stupid I had been trying something like that. I knew Mom would be so disappointed. She had done her best to keep me on the straight and narrow.

When we arrived at the juvenile hall I didn't know what to expect. I kept waiting for them to put me in a cell with all the wayward children that I had always heard ended up in places like that. Luckily, they never did take me any further than the front office. That's where I sat in a side chair and leafed through magazines. But I was too nervous to read anything because I knew my fate included getting locked up *and* getting the whooping of a lifetime.

I'm not sure what happened to Larry because they separated us when we arrived at the facility. In fact, that was the last time I ever saw him.

After about an hour Mom walked through the door. I could hear her voice even before I saw her face because as she entered the building she was greeted by the facility's director. He just so happened to be a man she had grown up and gone to school with. I could hear him say, "Renetta, girl, you're looking good. What brings you out this way?"

Mom answered, "I received a call that the police had brought my son here for shoplifting."

He then said, "Oh no, I'm sorry to hear that, but everything is going to be all right. Let's go in here and see what's going on."

When they entered the room where I was sitting with the administrative assistants, I burst into tears. I knew I had let Mom down. I also knew that I had embarrassed her in front of one of her old classmates. I may have forgotten a lot of things about that morning, but I'll never forget what Mom's friend said to me.

"Young man, I know you know better than this because I know your mama didn't raise you to be this way."

He continued, "I don't know what your problem is, young man, but you need to get it together or you're going to end up dead or in jail. How do you think that will make your mama feel?"

In my young life I'm sure I had done some things to embarrass my mother. But I'm also sure that all of them paled in comparison to being arrested for shoplifting. And to top it all off, the store manager and the person operating the juvenile facility both knew my mom.

The director then addressed me in a very stern voice.

"Son, this is your lucky day. Since this is your first offense, we are not going to lock you up. But we are going to write this incident up."

He said, "Tomorrow, your mama will have to take you to the city hall. They may have something different in mind, or they may go ahead and seal your records. It's all up to them."

I didn't know what "seal your records" meant, but it left me shaking in my boots. On the drive home I was waiting for some kind of backhand slap. But I knew that would only be the prelude to the beat down to come when I got home. That pain never came. Neither did the good old-fashioned cussing out that I was so sure would go along with the beating.

When we finally got home, I just sat on the porch because I knew what would be waiting inside. You see, Mom was the kind of mother who didn't mind whooping my butt, especially when I stepped out of line, sassed her, brought home bad grades or skipped out on something she wanted me to do. Therefore, I knew I had just been nominated to receive the "butt whooping" of a lifetime.

By then, all my friends had heard what happened and were stopping by trying to find out the details. Whenever Mom would see any of them out on the porch, she'd tell them through the glass storm door, "Baby, he can't have any company."

Still, I knew that beating was coming, so I kept sitting on the porch until it was almost dark. The whole time I was contemplating, should I stay and take it like a man or should I just take off and run away? But where was an 11-year-old kid with no money and only the clothes on his back to go?

As the sun began to set Mom finally opened the door and said, "You can come on in. I'm not going to whip you. But tomorrow, if they want to keep you, they just keep you."

That's when I lost it and burst into tears. Those words

hurt more than any beating ever could have. The next morning when we got to the city hall, they didn't arrest me. But they did seal my records, which made it seem like the incident never even happened, and I was free to go home. However, I was banned from ever stepping back into Dixie store again. Years had passed before I finally got up the nerve to show my face there. And since that fateful day I never tried anything as crazy as shoplifting again.

SIX

MEMPHIS BLUES AND ALL THAT JAZZ

AFTER ABOUT A year, Herman's gig in Memphis was winding down. Naturally, he was looking for somewhere else to work his craft. And it just so happened that the Aqua Lounge wanted him back in Birmingham. Herman had talent, style and charisma— all of the things it takes to seduce an audience into sitting in a smoke-filled room listening to a man make love to a saxophone as passionately as he'd make love to a woman.

Three weeks later, Herman was back in the Magic City, rocking the crowd at the Aqua with syncopated rhythms and smooth melodies on his horn. Mom hadn't worked there since he moved to Memphis. The club would close down about two o'clock every morning. But unlike before, Herman wasn't going home to his tricked-out apartment across town. Instead, he was coming home to our house, and, oh my God, did it shake things up.

I quickly learned that Herman was an alcoholic. His drink of choice was scotch. He'd chase it with soda, milk, water or sometimes he'd just take it straight up on ice. It was common for him to wake up and head straight for the bottle. You could find him nursing several drinks throughout the day. And yes, it was also part of his nighttime ritual, especially before and during his gigs.

Herman would often get so drunk that he'd come home about three o'clock in the morning, staggering into the house. He'd turn on his reel-to-reel tape player that had all of his favorite artists like John Coltrane, Nina Simone and Jothan Callins cued up. Herman would turn the volume up so loud that if it didn't wake you up, chances are you were already dead. It didn't seem to matter to him that I had to be in school or that Mom had to be at work early in the morning.

Many nights he'd come in talking loud about what a great night they had at the club or how bad things had been.

His recollections of the night always went from one extreme to another. He could be happy and jolly or rude and obnoxious. The conversations between him and Mom would go on and on for hours. He didn't stop talking until he'd eventually drink himself into a drunken stupor and fall asleep. By then, it was usually time for me and Mom to get up and start our day. Soon my grades began to drop because I'd find myself sleeping in class. So Mom had me to start studying more at night to boost my grades.

In Herman's defense, when he wasn't drunk he was more than just an outstanding father figure, he was also a friend. He'd spend quality time with the family on a regular basis. When I'd get home from school Herman was usually just waking up. He'd shower and dress, then we'd do something really interesting together like going to a movie, museum or a park until Mom got home from work.

Then we'd run back by the house to pick her up, and we'd go out to dinner if Herman hadn't already cooked. Morrison's Cafeteria in Eastwood Mall was their favorite place to eat during the week. It was a steam table diner where you'd grab a tray as you came in and worked your way down an assembly line, telling the servers what you wanted. They'd then plate it up and pass it to you through the glass that separated the food from the diners.

Whenever we went there I usually got the carrot and raisin salad, squash croquettes, baked chicken and a soft roll. Even to this day I still go for the carrot and raisin salad. After dinner, we'd head back to the house. I'd get Mom to check my homework, then take a bath and head to bed.

Mom and Herman would have their private time before it was time for him to head back to the Aqua Lounge. Everyone knew Herman exuded talent beyond measure. But for most of his life, the alcohol, marijuana, cocaine and other demons clouded his judgment when it came to making wise decisions.

I also think because he never quite made it into the big league he became bitter toward many of the people he had helped get to the top, none of whom reached back to pull him up with them. Herman's drunkenness had become part of a vicious cycle. In fact, it got to the point where it was downright embarrassing. One night, things got so bad that Mom tried to calm him down.

"Baby, you're still a great musician. People still love you, and night after night you pack the club with adoring fans."

He said, "Stop trying to appease me. My life is fucked up while all those bitches I've helped to get to the top couldn't give a damn about me."

"But, baby, you are making it," Mom said. "Everyone knows how great you are."

Herman shouted, "Just cut the bullshit, Renetta. As much as I've done for these motherfuckers, and they wanna treat me like this . . . like I'm no-fuckin'-body."

Herman was getting more and more agitated.

Mom said, "Baby, calm down."

"Bitch, don't tell me to calm the fuck down," he said. "Do you see how I have to put up with this shit? I already have to put up with this shit at the club, now I gotta come home and put up with this shit from you too?"

Once again Mom told him, "Baby, calm down."

Things really exploded when he told her, "Don't tell me to calm the fuck down. You calm your ass down."

Then he balled his fist and yelled, "Do you want some of this shit, huh? You want some of this shit?"

Again Mom said, "Herman, please calm down."

Mom must have felt seriously threatened at that moment because she came directly into my room and quietly told me to put my clothes on. The next thing I knew we were running to Aunt Von's house which was on the next street two blocks up. As we ran we kept looking back to see if Herman was chasing us.

He wasn't, but he was standing on the front porch in only his blue boxer shorts calling for us to come back. I could hear him screaming.

"You know I didn't mean it, baby, I'm sorry, come back."

But we just kept running.

I remember hearing our feet as they trampled the sidewalk and crossed the street. Dogs were barking and pacing their fenced in yards as we ran past their territory.

When we got to Aunt Von's, our adrenaline was so high that we weren't even exhausted from the unexpected sprint. However, I could tell Mom was afraid that Herman would drive up at any moment and cause a scene that would erupt into violence and chaos. I was scared.

My aunt's house was completely dark when we banged on the door and rang the doorbell repeatedly. It was apparent that we had awakened her and Uncle James because as they were opening the door they were also turning on lights, yawning and putting on their robes. They both had a surprised look of confusion on their face.

Aunt Von opened the door screaming, "Net, what's wrong?"

As we entered the house Mom said, "Girl, Herman is drunk and acting a fool. He threatened to hit me so I told Wayne to put his clothes on and let's go."

Mom was crying and shaking as Aunt Von helped her to the sofa. But Mom could not sit still. She knew the threat was not over. She used the yellow telephone that was affixed to the wall near the kitchen sink to call the police. The handheld receiver was attached to a coiled cord. It was long enough for her to talk to the officer and pace the entire kitchen floor with nervous energy. Aunt Von turned on the TV to steer my attention away from the drama unfolding. Ironically, she couldn't protect me from the *PTL Club*'s Tammy Faye Baker's mascara-stained tears plastered across the TV screen. Emotion was everywhere.

When the two police officers arrived at my aunt's house you could hear the constant chatter from the station dispatcher. It was coming through the handheld radios that were clipped to their belts. As Mom gave her account of what had just happened, I was fixated on their dark blue uniforms, hats, silver badges, handcuffs, black nightsticks and guns.

After taking Mom's statement they went around to our house and spoke with Herman. A short time later, the police came back to my aunt's house. They told Mom that Herman was calm and that he said he had no intention of hurting us.

When day broke we went home. Herman was apologetic to both of us and promised that he would never do that again. Months passed and I never saw him erupt back into that boiling monster; but with his constant drinking and drugging, there always seemed to be a sustained slow simmer that could reach its tipping point at any moment, especially if the temperature was turned up just a little bit.

Through all of that ugliness, Mom continued her journey with Herman. I guess love will make you do some crazy things. And even though I hated what Herman did to Mom, I never hated him. In fact, I loved him and continued to have a deep respect and appreciation for his talent and intelligence. I somehow understood him better. But I pitied the man whose life was now haunted by his past.

Musicians often seem to have a life on the run. After about 2 years in Birmingham, Herman was asked to return to Memphis to put a band together for a popular nightclub owner at the Holiday Inn Rivermont. It was a swanky, luxury hotel that sat on the banks of the Mississippi River and was famous for its celebrity clientele.

You could look out from some of the rooms and watch dozens of barges carrying their loads up and down that old muddy river. If you happened to be there at just the right time, you could get a glimpse of the great *Mississippi Queen*.

The *Mississippi Queen* was at one time the world's second-largest paddle-driven steamboat. It carried more than 400 passengers all the way down the river from Cincinnati to New Orleans for a luxury cruise filled with food, frolic and libations. The passengers could be seen standing out on the New Orleans-style balconies. They'd wave to the crowds that stood along the riverbanks as the paddle boat passed the Memphis skyline.

Before making the transition to Memphis, home to Stax Records, Beale Street, Elvis Presley and the Church of God in Christ, Mom and Herman exchanged wedding vows in a private ceremony. She kept her old married name of Gray. She said she continued to use that name because she had accepted a job as an event booking agent at the same hotel where Herman was working. That way, they could avoid any possible conflict of interest.

We moved into a really nice suburb just north of Memphis called Raleigh. The condominium complex had two swimming pools, a beautiful lake, large bedrooms and a cozy clubhouse. But because it was so far out it wasn't convenient to much of anything. In fact, it took at least an hour to get from the condo to downtown Memphis where Mom and Herman both worked.

Because the commute was so far it would be difficult to get to me if anything happened at school. So I came up with the idea that I should just stay in town with Andrea and Tonya along with Daddy and Mother Green. I begged Mom to let me stay there.

They were the only people I really knew in Memphis besides the friends I had met on Texas Street over the past couple of years. Plus, deep down, I really didn't want to have to put up with Herman's drinking night after night.

I guess since Mom didn't really know the big city either she agreed. She knew the area where Andrea lived, including churches and schools, very well. I ended up staying with Andrea and attending Lincoln Junior High School. I'd have to wake up every morning to catch a school bus to get there, but I looked forward to it. Even though I had been forced to grow up quickly, staying with Andrea helped me to develop an even greater sense of independence. It was during that time that I started discovering new things about myself. Like the fact that I loved all types of music, clothes and boys. Even though I knew I was attracted to boys as early as the third grade, I never acted upon it.

But when I began eighth grade at Lincoln Junior High School, I met a guy named Theo. He was tall, dark and slender with a muscular build. Although he had the usual skin blemishes that so many teens our age would get, it didn't matter. He exuded a certain amount of sex appeal that captured my attention. My heart would actually flutter whenever I'd see him in class or walking down the hall. Not only was I attracted to him physically but also spiritually. He was honest, had a pure heart and loved God. He was a member of the Church of God in Christ which forged an instant bond between us.

Theo and I never ever messed around with as much as a kiss, but I knew we had a vibe that I hadn't felt for a man before. I think the only reason we never acted upon our feelings is because we only interacted at school. We weren't old enough to drive, and we lived so far apart that it wouldn't have been possible to even walk to each other's house.

However, we talked on the phone constantly and fantasized about all the things we thought we wanted to do with each other. Theo was my first puppy love crush. And even though it was with a boy, it never felt strange, just natural. Still, we kept it a secret for fear of being ridiculed or even beat up.

During that time, being gay was not nearly accepted as it is now.

Staying in the same town as my mother but living on Texas Street about an hour away was never what I expected. In some ways, I liked it because I had a freedom with Andrea that I never would have had with my mother. Although we talked on the phone every day and spent weekends together, I missed her dearly.

When summer rolled around, Herman packed Mom, Tonya and me up in his gold Buick and took us on a road trip to New Jersey. We went to pick up his daughter Terri who was a couple of years younger than I. Riding in a car from Tennessee to New Jersey was quite an experience. It was my first real vacation, but it seemed like it took forever to get there. I can remember reading all of the highway signs and singing every tune that played on the radio as we rolled our way across the state of Tennessee.

As we began approaching the Great Smoky Mountains all you could hear in the car were "Ooo's" and "Ah's."

That unbroken chain of mountains was so tall that it looked like they were making their way into the heavens. But the valleys that lay between them were just as breathtaking. Like me, everybody in the car perked up and stared at the sides of the road, hoping to get a glimpse of some wild animals like deer, elks or coyotes, but we never did.

After arriving in D.C., we made a car tour of the White House, U.S. Capitol, Washington Monument and other notable exhibits on the National Mall. And we made a quick stop to eat at a D.C. soul food restaurant.

It must have been about 11:30 that night when we finally arrived at Terri's house. We stayed in the car while Herman went in to get my new stepsister. We all greeted her with hugs and kisses. Herman squeezed her suitcases into the trunk with the rest of our things.

Terri was a beautiful girl with a warm spirit. Her mother was a Caucasian jazz singer and ballerina. Of course, her father was an exceptional musician that could charm the snakes out of a basket and not get bitten. Nonctheless, my stepsister says she didn't inherit the talents of either of her parents.

Terri and I had met once before when she and Tonya made a visit to Birmingham during the Christmas break. But this time, I was looking forward to getting to know her better and bonding as brother and sister.

After picking Terri, up we headed toward the George Washington Bridge to make our way into New York City. It must have been about one o'clock in the morning when we got there, about 24 hours after we left Memphis. With all the flashing billboards, bustling cars and crowds of people lining the streets and sidewalks, it made it all seem like five o'clock in the afternoon in the middle of rush-hour traffic.

Our visit to New York City just happened to be around the time that the notorious killer named the "Son of Sam" was roaming the streets. The so-called Son of Sam was being stalked by law officials for his role in the murders of several women in the New York City area.

Finally, Terri, Tonya and I got settled into our hotel room. Mom and Herman were staying in the adjacent room. Even though we were on the twenty-first floor, it was still haunting to think that a serial killer was on the prowl and could be right outside our door.

We stayed in New York for about a week. Of course, we saw all the sights, including the Statue of Liberty, Empire State Building, Brooklyn Tunnel, Harlem, Chinatown, Coney Island, Dodger Stadium, the World Trade Center and Times Square where they always throw a big party to ring in the New Year.

We even saw the Macy's Fourth of July fireworks display on the Hudson River. It was even bigger and brighter than the Thunder on the Mountain Fourth of July display in Birmingham that I still love to this day.

Even as a teenager I summed up New York City as a nice place to visit but not anyplace I'd like to live. The streets were too busy, the waits in lines to get into anywhere were too long, and the cost of living was way too expensive. Herman took us to visit a musician friend who was renting a studio apartment in Manhattan. I know it had to have been the size of a standard hospital room. And in the mid-'70s he was paying close to $2,000 a month for that little bit of real estate.

While I enjoyed visiting New York City, it couldn't compare with the joy I got from traveling to upstate New York and seeing the mighty Niagara Falls. To this day, it has to be at the top of my list of the most romantic places in the world. There is something to be said about the natural awe and beauty of the falls. In fact, a visit back there is near the top of my bucket list.

SEVEN

HOME IS WHERE THE HEART IS

"WE ARE FAMILY" is a dance hit made popular by the group Sister Sledge. It's a song I've been singing with my two step-sisters for years.

When our family vacation ended I was looking forward to spending some quality time in Memphis with them before heading to Birmingham. So Terri and I both stayed with Andrea up on Texas Street. She was the glue that kept the Green family together. Andrea was Mother and Elder Green's caregiver. She was also the go-to person for anything concerning matters within their household.

Andrea would take us everywhere with her, including her late-night runs to a Fred Montesis Grocery Store on the other side of town. That's where she'd purchase a particular cheese, yogurt or certain cut of meat or fish. She'd also take us to the Muhammad Ali Theater to hear her friends, the Bar-Kays and

Con Funk Shun perform in concert. That was just before the two groups became international superstars.

Andrea was a member of Bountiful Blessings Church, and she often took us with her. The pastor was Apostle Gilbert Earl Patterson, nephew of Bishop J. O. Patterson who was at that time the presiding bishop of the Church of God in Christ. Gilbert Earl had just left COGIC to start a more contemporary church that welcomed people from all walks of life.

His philosophy was "Come as you are." Apostle G. E. Patterson welcomed everybody, from prostitutes to politicians to drug dealers who had nearly given up on God and religion.

It didn't matter if you were in a three-piece suit or blue jeans and a tee shirt. His message was so powerful that the first Sunday he opened the doors of his two-story brownstone church, he took in over a hundred members. Since then, his membership had grown to include thousands of people from across Memphis and surrounding areas. The service was energetic and very much in the charismatic order of COGIC. But the overall atmosphere was more relaxed and perhaps less judgmental.

Bountiful Blessings sat on a corner near one of the city's most depressed neighborhoods. However, once inside, the crystal chandeliers and plush green cushions that padded the pews made the sanctuary look like the finer churches in town. Bountiful Blessings had become the "it" church for people who didn't typically think of church as being cool. In addition, their community outreach programs that fed, clothed and paid utility bills for thousands of people made the Bible-based church a beacon of hope for hundreds of area residents.

Andrea was heavily involved in the Bountiful Blessing movement. She served as a pulpit assistant. Come Thursday night, Sunday morning and Sunday night Andrea would have

Terri, Tonya and me in church. I loved everything about Bountiful Blessings, including the preaching and singing. But what really caught my attention was the young man who introduced the church as their radio broadcast was coming on the air. His voice was so rich and commanding that it instantly caught my attention and I wanted to sound just like him. I would capture his voice on my cassette tape recorder and listen to him repeatedly. I'd listen to that tape nearly every day and try to imitate his distinct character and flair. Even then, I knew I wanted to do exactly what he was doing.

Terri, Tonya and I had gotten so familiar with the church that we used to come home and imitate the way certain members shouted or sang or preached. They still talk about how I used to go around the house preaching and laying hands on them until they would shout or fall out as if they were slain in the Spirit.

Little did I know so much of what I was learning back then I would come to rely on in the years ahead. I am so glad to say today that I am still a believer in Jesus. And I believe that he continues to use ordinary people to do extraordinary things. And, yes, it is still my desire to be used by him.

When the time had come to say good-bye to my sisters and board the bus for Birmingham, I was more than a little saddened. In that short amount of time we had grown so close. We didn't have the modern conveniences of the Internet or cell phones at that time. However, I knew our hearts would always be connected wherever life would take us.

The bus ride to Birmingham began just like all of the other rides I'd taken over the years. The driver would stop in nearly every town to pick up one or two passengers here and there. We stopped in some of the strangest places. Sometimes the pickup location was an old-fashioned service station similar to where Goober worked on TV's, *The Andy Griffith Show*. One stop was a restaurant named Mel's Diner. No joke, Mel's Diner.

Occasionally, we'd stop at an actual Greyhound Bus terminal where passengers could transfer to a bus headed in another direction. But this particular day something happened that I had never seen before. We were riding along a country highway somewhere between Sulligent and Jasper, Alabama. The driver began making a sudden stop along the side of the road. All you could see was a long stretch of highway surrounded by trees and hills. I looked hard to see if there was a building, a lamppost or even a sign that said Greyhound or anything similar hidden behind the trees. But I didn't see one.

As I looked out the window I saw a small group of people that seemed to be a family gathered together. The gentleman appeared to be in his early 40s, the woman about the same age. A teenage boy was dressed in blue jeans and a black T-shirt with a peace sign on it. There was a pecan-complexioned woman with them. I pegged her to be in her early 20s, and she was dressed to the nines.

She had on a yellow-fitted sleeveless dress that perfectly molded to her hourglass silhouette. Her hair was pulled back and rolled into a ball with a white orchid pinned to the side. Her makeup was so flawless that it looked like she had just stepped away from a session with a fashion fair cosmetics consultant.

When the bus driver pulled in front of them I could see her hugging and kissing the others good-bye. As the door opened, the beautiful young woman gently picked up her light brown suitcase. Gracefully stepping onto the bus, she flashed a great big smile that showed the prettiest white teeth I'd ever seen.

But it was what she said in a loud distinctive Southern drawl that shocked the show.

"YOU IS GOING TO BIRMINGHAM, AIN'T YA?"

The whole bus laughed in delight. It's a memory that has stayed with me forever. It's one of those rare moments that will never come around again. But it's a moment that has made me laugh for years every time I think about it. I've often wondered about that young woman. Was she a fashion model heading somewhere in search of her big break? Or was she a college student heading off to get a degree in hopes of making the world a better place? Chances are slim to none that I'll ever know the answers to those questions. What I do know is that she stirred a desire in me to someday say something that would touch the hearts and souls of people, touch them in a positive way that they would never forget.

Stepping off of the Greyhound Bus onto the streets of Birmingham was like taking in a breath of fresh air. It felt good being home, surrounded by friends, loved ones and familiar territory. The day I arrived, Aunt Von and Uncle James were throwing a big old-fashioned backyard barbecue. It's something our family would regularly do just to maintain our closeness.

While Uncle James was standing in front of the slightly rusted barbecue grill that he had made out of an old barrel, I could see plumes of hickory-flavored smoke rising from its pit. As he turned the slabs of pork ribs, chicken wings, hamburgers and smoked sausages you could hear the music as meat met heat.

"Ahhh! Shhh! Taaa! Shooo!"

Those were the sounds of the juices dripping down on the hot, burning coals. Every now and then, it would spark a flame that would crawl its way up to the grill. Those flames seared in the tender, juicy flavor of every morsel of meaty goodness. And the sweet smells filled the air.

By early evening the party was in full swing with family and friends fully engaged in a fierce game of badminton. In between rounds, James Jr., Edwin and I would take turns cranking the handle on the old-fashioned wooden bucket ice cream freezer and adding ice and rock salt to keep it good and cold. We had to take turns because cranking that old freezer wore our arms out after just a few minutes of churning. Homemade ice cream has been a family tradition at our summertime gatherings for years. After about an hour of cranking, Aunt Von sent out the call.

"Who wants ice cream?"

Everyone stopped whatever they were doing just to get a scoop of that summertime goodness. We'd sit around the wooden deck, eating ice cream, shooting the breeze, cracking a few jokes and catching up on the latest happenings.

The party finally ended about ten o'clock that night. The dishes had been washed, and all of the trash taken out. All we had left to do was get our clothes ready for Sunday school and church the next day, take our showers and head to bed.

James Jr., Edwin and I shared a room. I was the oldest, Edwin the youngest and there was a 4-year difference between each of us.

Edwin and James Jr. had the bunk beds with James taking the top bunk. Their dresser separated them from my twin bed, and a television sat on a chest of drawers across the room near the foot of my bed.

Our bedroom had the typical boy motif—blue walls, hardwood floors and posters of our favorite football, basketball and music heroes.

Deirdre's room was like something out of a fairy tale. Her

bed was draped in an ivory canopy that spanned from the ceiling to the floor. The walls were a soft shade of pink flanked with an ivory-colored dresser that a huge gold-trimmed mirror hung above. Dozens of teddy bears and dolls lined her bed. And a fully furnished dollhouse custom built by Uncle James comfortably sat in its own corner of the room. She often had pretend tea parties with all of her plush little friends, including Michael, a teddy bear that she has kept in her possession even into adulthood.

Aunt Von and Uncle James's bedroom was up the hall off the living room and across from my aunt's sewing room. It was fairly modest with a king-sized bed, but what I remember most is Aunt Von's shoe collection. She had so many shoes that they couldn't all fit in her closet, so she'd line them all up in their boxes and stack them along the bedroom walls. Uncle James seemed content to have one hall closet for himself.

James Jr., Edwin and I spent most of that night catching up on the past year before we eventually fell asleep. The next morning we woke up to Uncle James's call.

"You knuckleheads better get y'all's tails out of bed. It's time to get ready for church."

As I opened my eyes I could hear the sound of pots and pans and eggs being cracked open and beaten with a wire whisk. From her always-present glass bowl, Aunt Von would pour the mixture into a sizzling hot skillet. I'd make it into the kitchen in time to see her stir the mixture around with a metal spatula until they were softly scrambled.

After eating a hearty breakfast, we assembled in the living room where we knelt around the coffee table. Uncle James led us in family prayer by praising God for simply being God. He also thanked him for keeping us safe and sound through the night, and he asked him to keep us as we journeyed through the day. That's the way every day would begin at my aunt and uncle's house.

After a year in Memphis it felt good returning to my Eleventh Avenue church family. When we arrived at church, everyone welcomed me back with open arms. I went right back to singing in the choir and serving as a junior superintendent of our Sunday school. After church, we all went home, ate dinner, and because it was Edwin's turn to do the dishes that day, he was left in the kitchen. Deirdre, James Jr. and I chilled in our bedrooms watching TV and listening to music. Aunt Von was extremely religious and didn't allow secular music to be played in her home. The only music we could listen to was either classical or gospel. One of her favorite groups was Andraé Crouch and the Disciples. At that time Andraé Crouch was a rising star who was forging a fresh contemporary sound in gospel music. His latest release was a huge hit called "Take Me Back."

Aunt Von gave me a copy of the album, and I instantly fell in love with all of his music. Through his music I could hear all of the syncopated rhythms that I had come to love from secular artists like Earth, Wind and Fire, Stevie Wonder and Aretha Franklin. But beyond that, it was through his music and ministry that I realized young people could look cool and hip and still be Christian.

Crouch wrote what I call love songs to God. Each one of them expressed so many of the thoughts I felt in my heart about the Creator. The very first song on that album was called "I'll Still Love You." The words were a simple expression of everything I was feeling. It's as if he knew me.

"Even when the cold winds blow, dear Lord, I want you to know I'll still love you, Lord, I'll still love you. Nothing shall ever separate me from your love . . . Nothing on earth below or nothing above."

I believed that then, and I still believe it now because even in my darkest hours God has faithfully been there to see me through. That summer I bought a couple more Andraé Crouch albums. In fact, I spent the majority of my free time listening to every lyric, beat and rhythm of his songs. Anyone who knows me also knows that even to this day I'm probably his number one fan.

I spent the rest of that summer bonding with each member of my family in our own unique way. Still I couldn't stop thinking about Mom and wondering if she was doing OK. But I'll always be especially grateful for the quality time I spent with Uncle James. Right from the start he took me in as if I was his own son. And I came to love him like a father. My uncle was a metal craftsman by trade and worked at a mill called Conner's Steel. But Uncle James was really a jack-of-all-trades and master of many. He was an excellent carpenter, plumber, heating and air-conditioning repairman. You name it he could do it. However, his favorite passion was reupholstering old pieces of furniture. He could breathe new life into old sofas and chairs by restoring them back to their original glory.

I spent a lot of time in his backyard upholstery shop. On the outside it was a garage. But on the inside, the ceiling was lined with bolts of fabric resting across the exposed beams.

On the walls were cabinets filled with a variety of threads in nearly every color of the rainbow. Rolls of brown-corded webbing, boxes of buttons and mountains of white foam padding all had a place in the shop. Three florescent light fixtures hung from the ceiling illuminating the entire room. And there was a little portable radio on top of a metal shelf near my uncle's sewing machine. The local gospel music radio station could always be heard playing in the background. But that old radio was in constant competition with Uncle James's industrial-strength sewing machine. That machine could make as many syncopated beats as world-renowned drummers like Max Roach and Sheila E. I loved the way it sounded as it stitched the pieces of fabric together into one masterpiece.

Whenever we picked up a new piece to work on, we would set it on a giant worktable in the middle of the room.

I'd help Uncle James remove the fabric and padding. Then he'd see if the wooden frame was secure. He'd fix the legs or arms that needed to be repaired or replaced. And if the coil springs were in good enough shape to be reused, he'd clean them up, good as new.

Together, we'd measure, cut and fit the coverings on what was being transformed into something completely new. As we began assembling the pieces back together, you could hear the shop come to life.

"*Screw, screw, screw, screw.*"

"*Tap, tap, tap, tap.*"

"*Tata, tata, tata, tata.*"

"*Zzzz, zzzz, zzzz, zzzz.*"

We made our own music as we screwed, stapled and tucked the fabric to the side, backs and bottoms of the piece. With cushions and pillows in place, that old outdated chair or sofa perked up with a new lease on life.

The garage upholstery shop was a special place where my uncle and I talked nearly every day. He taught me how to restore the luster to an old piece of furniture that had seen its better days. But he also shared life lessons that would carry me into manhood. Uncle James is the one who taught me about sex and unwanted teenage pregnancies.

"Son, a woman's body is a temple, and so is yours; take care of it. You're getting toward that age when you're going to want to experiment with sex, but I am here to tell you you're not ready yet," he said.

Uncle James seemed to be searching for the right words to say, and when he finally found them it sounded something like this.

"Son, I'm not telling you to have sex. In fact, I want you to wait until you're married. But if you should find yourself in that situation, please, please, please use a condom."

He said, "Besides having a baby that you can't afford, you could also catch a sexually transmitted disease. And I know you don't want anything like syphilis, gonorrhea or herpes."

In addition to teaching me about the pitfalls of sex, he also taught me the importance of always being a gentleman. He said being polite would take me a long way in life.

"Make it a habit to hold the door open not only for women but also for men and children."

I can still hear him saying, "Pull a woman's seat out as she is about to sit down."

And he told me to always open the car door and extend a hand to a lady as she enters or exits a vehicle.

"Wayne, you're almost 15 and you'll be getting your driver's permit soon. When you start driving, please don't pull up to a young lady's house and blow your car horn for her to come out. Don't even do that for a man. Have enough courtesy to go ring the doorbell."

Uncle James also taught me the importance of keeping my word.

"A man's word is his bond. If you say you're going to do something, do it."

And he taught me about being honest.

"If you can't do it, just say, 'I'm sorry, I thought I could do it, but I can't.'"

He taught me to always be a leader not a follower, to always respect my elders and to give the first 10 percent of everything I earned to God. The next 10 percent he said I should pay myself by putting it in the bank.

Uncle James gave me so many useful tools, including one Mom had given me through the years. It was a quote by William Shakespeare.

"To thine own self be true."

Putting it in Uncle James's terms, "If you mess up, fess up." He said, "People respect a man who owns his own stuff, be it good or bad."

Again, I am reminded that it does indeed take a village to raise a child.

What do you have when you combine First Lady Michelle Obama, Mother Teresa and Martha Stewart all into one?

Aunt Von.

She was the first person in my family that I knew to go to college. Uncle James paid for every one of her classes out of his own pocket. So when she graduated with honors from the University of Alabama at Birmingham (UAB), they didn't have to worry about paying back thousands of dollars in student loans. Aunt Von graduated with degrees in mass communications and early childhood education.

Growing up, I remember how challenging it was for her to balance school while taking care of her family. There were many weekends when my mom would want her to go shopping or run an errand with her. But Aunt Von couldn't because she was busy studying. There were many times when Mom and I would stop by my aunt's house and she would be lying in bed surrounded by books and papers. She was studying for an exam or trying to complete an assignment by class time.

When I came to stay with them that summer, Aunt Von

was well into her career. She was a third-grade teacher at Glen Iris Elementary School, which was one of the better schools in Birmingham. Even though she was a dedicated and well respected educator, by summer break she was ready to do some of the things she missed during the year.

Aunt Von and Uncle James were perfect for each other. He loved upholstery work, and she loved antiques. That summer she and I often woke up early on Saturday mornings. We'd make our rounds to dozens of garage and estate sales looking for antique furniture, china and vintage clothing. Her living room was decorated with a number of antiques that she had found at those sales and Uncle James brought back to life. Aunt Von had many prized possessions, including a Duncan Phyfe sofa, but her love for antiques also extended to anything eclectic and eccentric. She told me that she loved collecting things that evoked a story saying, "When I look at a piece I wonder why it survived." It was the lure of the story that drew her into antiques.

She said she'd wanted to know why people took care of a particular piece and preserved it through the years. She wondered what made it special to the person who owned it, asking, "Was it the curve of the wood, the fabric or a memory?"

While Aunt Von had an eye for furnishings, she also had a flair for fashion. And, oh my God, could she make a dress pop. She was about 5 foot 9 and could wear a suit or dress as well as any fashion model working the runway.

Even with her style and sense of fashion, Aunt Von remained one of the most humble and caring people I'd ever known. I've never even heard her engage in gossip, malice or bitterness with anyone. She was an extremely loving and gentle woman who believed in the power of God and prayer.

My aunt loved beautiful clothes and home furnishings, but we both shared a love for journalism.

Even though she enjoyed teaching, what she really wanted to be was a network television news journalist. However, she said with all the traveling and long hours involved she didn't believe it was a practical career for a married woman with children.

I adored everything about my aunt. And even though I was only her nephew she would always include me as her son whenever she was introducing her children. I felt right at home with their family.

Over the short span of that warm summer I found myself assuming the role of big brother for my cousins James Jr., Edwin and Deirdre. I loved them beyond measure, and we all seemed to make a perfect fit. When summer finally came to an end and the time had come for me to go back to Memphis, my family and I had what I call a Gladys Knight moment. I get that saying from her hit song, "Neither One of Us."

I certainly didn't want to leave. And even though my little cousins may not have articulated it directly, I could see the same feelings in their eyes. They were gonna miss having me around to play basketball with them the backyard. I was sure Edwin would miss the way my best friend Ernest and I would pick him up by his legs and arms and glide him through the air like he was a human swing. And yes, I knew James Jr. would miss having me there to lighten his load of cleaning up the kitchen and weekly household chores.

I was going to miss things too, like reading to Deirdre. Some of the stories were the same ones her mother had read to me when I was her age.

A week before Mom was supposed to drive down to take me back to Memphis I threw a wrench in the plans. I asked

Aunt Von and Uncle James if I could stay with them and go to school in Birmingham. Of course, I didn't realize it at the time how much of a responsibility it would be for them to have a high school freshman living under their roof.

But based on conversations with Uncle James years later, it was a call they welcomed right from the start. He said they saw potential in me that needed to be nourished, and he said they knew they could help me tap into it. Uncle James told me that from the very beginning they knew they could provide me with the stable environment that I needed to help me grow.

My aunt and uncle were very familiar with the late-night disturbances that I'd had to endure living with my mother and jazz musician stepfather. Uncle James told me that from the moment I asked to stay with them they were on board. The hardest part however, was selling Mom on the idea. Our phone conversation went something like this.

"Mom, you know I love you, right?"

"Of course, son, and you know I love you too, so what's going on?"

"Mom, I really like it here. I miss being with my friends and all of my family. Plus, I really want to go to high school with all of my friends that I've grown up with."

"Son, you have friends here. And I love you and want you here with me."

"I know, Mom, and I love you too. I want to be with you too. But, Herman . . . Mom, I can't take all the drinking and cursing and late nights. And I don't like the way he talks to you. Plus, I can tell that he really doesn't want me there."

"Son, that's not true."

"Mom, maybe it's not true, but it feels like it."

Mom made a long sigh. "Uhhhh." She asked, "Have you talked about this with Von and James?"

"Yes, ma'am, and they want me to stay."

Mom began crying on the phone. "Son, I only want what's best for you. But I don't know about this."

I had tears in my eyes, and my heart was beating fast.

She then said, "I want you to be happy. But my sister can't see after you and take care of her own children too."

"Mom, they want me to stay. Plus, they say I'll be an asset to them too by helping look after the kids."

"I don't know, son, I'll have to really pray about this."

"This doesn't mean I don't love you, Mom. And I promise to come stay with you every holiday and summer."

After days of begging and pleading from me, along with hours of conversations with Aunt Von and Uncle James, she finally signed off on the plan.

Even though my family allowed me to move to Birmingham, my uncle told me it wasn't because they didn't respect my mother. But he did say they knew she was young and still finding herself. He said they wanted to help her any way they could, even helping her son grow into a man.

Uncle James also let me know that the decision to let me stay didn't have any reflection on Herman. In fact, my whole family loved and appreciated Herman for his talent, charm and charisma. Herman was even part of the reason my cousin Deirdre decided to study music in addition to engineering. However, they did understand his addiction and how it could affect him and those around him, especially a young, impressionable teenager.

In its earlier days, Carroll W. Hayes High School had been known for its stellar band, competitive athletics and alumni that read like a list of Who's Who. A list filled with attorneys, doctors, educators, professional athletes, musicians, building contractors, even journalists. But like the middle-class homes and brick government projects it was nestled between, Hayes had seen better days.

The family didn't want me to go to Hayes. They wanted me to attend one of the local private or alternative schools. But because of the logistics in getting me there they agreed to allow me to start at Hayes, then transfer to another school my sophomore year, after I'd gotten my driver's license.

Hayes was near one of the most notorious housing projects in Birmingham. It had the potential to be a mini version of the school from the movie, *Lean on Me*. And like in the movie, Hayes's saving grace was its principal. J. B. Norman had been the principal since the days when my mom graduated from there shortly after I was born. Behind his back we all affectionately called him J. B.

J. B. ran a no-nonsense kind of school.

I always appreciated his hands-on approach because it made me feel safe. He didn't tolerate tardiness, hoodlums or failure. He insisted that everything was done orderly. And he demanded excellence, not only from his students but also his instructors.

The campus was a good 30-minute walk from my house. But it was a walk that I took with plenty of company. Most were friends from Dupuy Elementary School.

During my first year of high school, I played drums in the band and sang in the school choir. And while I'd always felt that I was smart and talented, that year I discovered new things about myself.

I found out that I danced to the beat of a different drummer. I began interacting with people from all walks of life and could fit into almost any group. That included girls from the upper echelon with the long pretty hair and noses in the air and the guys who stood on the corner shooting the breeze about sports, girls and dreams.

I felt pretty good about myself too. I had finally lost my baby fat, and I could wear an Afro just as well as Michael Jackson or Don Cornelius. I must admit I liked it when the girls ran their fingers through it.

Even though most people say I look just like my mom, she always said the older I got the more I looked like my father. All of those things helped to boost my confidence.

I think the kids liked my sense of humor, personal style and willingness to listen to their problems without being judgmental. They also trusted me because they knew they could count on me to keep their secrets.

One of the most important things that I discovered about myself in high school is that I could tell a story in a way that captured people's attention. Just knowing that fueled my desire to use my voice to make people think.

During my sophomore year a speech instructor asked me to enter an oratorical contest. It was sponsored by the Inner City Jaycees of Birmingham. I honestly cannot recall the teacher's name. But I do remember she was a short, blond lady with a heart of gold and an ear for talent. The contest was part of a black history event.

To participate, you had to write and deliver a speech on the topic of black contributions to American society. I wrote the speech, but my cousin Delois, who was a sophomore at Talladega College, helped me tweak it. We'd work on my delivery when she came home on weekends. She would make me practice it for hours, critiquing my every word, every move, down to the moments I was supposed to pause and look at an audience member. It's been years since I gave that first speech, but I still remember a good portion of it even to this day.

Black contributions to American society is much

too broad to be fully discussed in the time allotted to us today.

Therefore, rather than focusing my attention on those so-called household names of American black society, I will place my emphasis on those contributors who are less well-known to us in the black community.

Names like James Baldwin, Countee Cullen, Gwendolyn Brooks, men and women who have very definitely been instrumental in creating the harmony which now exists.

The competition was held one Tuesday night at the main library downtown. Most of the contestants were juniors and seniors. I may have been the only sophomore.

Was I nervous?

If shaky knees and sweaty hands are any indication that a man is nervous, I was. When I finished the speech, the audience exploded with applause. After a few tense moments of deliberation, the judges finally made their big announcement.

"The grand prize winner is Lawayne Childrey from Hayes High School!"

Aunt Von, Uncle James and their kids stood to their feet as the rest of the audience followed their lead.

It was my night.

I had a trophy, a check for five hundred dollars and the respect of a room full of people for doing something I would have done for free. But having my family there cheering me on gave me the courage I needed to reach for even greater dreams.

At the beginning of my junior year, I joined the Distributive Education Clubs of America, also known as DECA. The club is an international association of marketing students whose goal is to help prepare emerging leaders and entrepreneurs in marketing, finance, hospitality and management. I only became a member because my best friend TJ asked me to join. TJ and I met at Hayes. As with most of my friends he was a year ahead of me.

Every year, DECA had a series of local, state and national competitions. The winners at the local and state levels would go on to compete at the national competition, which is always held in a beautiful hotel in an exotic U.S. city. The challenge was to merchandise an item giving written and oral details of how the product would be made and eventually sold.

Each contestant in my event had to give the marketing strategy, including overall cost and profit margins.

At the time, I was working part-time as a salesman at Kinney Shoes. So I chose to merchandise one of their leather handbags. I spent weeks on the project, including dozens of long nights and weekends. It eventually paid off because I ended up winning the state championship in my event. TJ won in his event, which automatically placed us in the national competition which was held in Miami, Florida, that summer.

It was my first time in Miami, and we stayed at the Fontainebleau Hilton. At that time, the Fontainebleau was one of the most luxurious hotels on Miami Beach. Anyone who was anyone, from Hollywood royalty to political heavyweights, stayed at the Fontainebleau. Mrs. Ham, our team adviser and mentor, had her own room on the seventh floor. Our teammates Angela and Constance shared a room on the twelfth floor, and TJ and I shared a room on the seventeenth floor, which was actually a bedroom in the Presidential Suite.

Fortunately for us, the bedroom air conditioner was not working properly, so the hotel staff unlocked the door separating our room from the rest of the suite to allow air to flow through. That meant we had total access to one of the most elegant suites in the entire hotel.

Being the outgoing aggressive type, TJ was in hog heaven. He started inviting everybody over to get a glimpse of our oceanfront view. I was the more reserved one, but I usually ended up getting suckered into his crazy antics. While TJ was partying it up one day, I was obsessing over a guy that had caught my attention on day one of the competition. He was part of the Tennessee delegation participating in the contest.

Over the years I had developed some great friendships with some of the most beautiful, sophisticated young ladies from school and church. And even though I had been intimate with a couple of them, the relationships never went beyond heavy petting. However, what I was feeling for this guy, whom I had never met, sent chills through my body unlike anything I had ever experienced before.

I had been watching him throughout the weeklong competition but was too shy to say anything. With a couple of days of competition left, I finally got up the nerve to introduce myself. In the hotel lobby, I walked up to him, struck up a conversation and we quickly became friends.

Knox Cowan was from Nashville. He was a year older than I, stood about 5 feet 8 and had smooth brown skin and big brown eyes. Knox had a small, well-defined frame, and I found his hairy arms, legs, thick eyebrows and long lashes to be extremely sexy.

I also liked the way he carried himself in a cool, calm, sophisticated way. He was well versed and had an impeccable eye for fashion.

At the end of the day, after our perspective teams had finished dinner and talked about how things were coming with our programs, Knox and I would meet up by the pool. We'd take long, romantic walks on the beach, talking about everything from school, to career goals, to our families. There was an instant chemistry between us. I don't know if it was because of the way the moon glowed across the ocean or the way the waves rolled along the shore soaking our bodies as we sat by the sea. All I know for sure is that when I looked into his eyes I could see eternity. The kiss of his lips was the sweetest I had ever tasted.

In just those couple of days that I spent with Knox, an impression of what I thought love should look like and feel like was forever etched in my mind. The night before my team headed back to Birmingham, Knox and I stayed on the beach all night until the sun came up. While I was honored to have placed in the top 3 percent of the competition, the highlight of the tournament was meeting Knox.

While saying our good-byes, we vowed to stay in touch through letters and phone calls. I didn't want to leave his warm and tender embrace, but I had to pack my bags, shower and meet my team in the lobby.

As the five-member Birmingham team crammed into a taxi for the airport, I knew I was going home a slightly different man than when I left.

EIGHT

WALKING IN MEMPHIS

I WOULD ONLY be in Birmingham a few days before heading to Memphis to live with Mom.

I drove there in my first car, a 1974 Ford Maverick. I bought it with the money I was making at Kinney Shoes, along with help from Mom and Uncle James. It was a muscle car that loved the road as much as I did.

Even though I would spend Thanksgiving, Christmas and summer breaks with Mom, this move was extra special because it would be the last year we'd spend together before I started college at the University of Tennessee at Chattanooga. I was even excited about spending time with Herman.

Mom and Herman were now living in a cozy little brick home in a predominately middle-class community in metropolitan Memphis called Whitehaven.

Mom had attended night school and received a degree in

business. She was working full time at the Holiday Inn corporate headquarters and part time at a telephone answering service.

Mother and Daddy Green had both passed away and Tonya and Andrea were now living in Chicago.

Herman was teaching jazz composition at LeMoyne-Owen College by day and playing the clubs at night.

Twice a week Herman met with his students at LeMoyne-Owen, which is one of the country's historically black colleges and universities. The campus was in the heart of one of the city's most depressed neighborhoods. But inside its gates students were gaining a wealth of knowledge through the dissemination of everything from physics to literature to music. Sometimes I'd go sit in on Herman's classes.

I can still remember him dressed in all-black sitting on a wooden stool in front of a small group of students. They sat in a semicircle of old wood and iron desks, asking a collage of questions. It was fascinating to watch and listen as Herman talked about his passion. He explained how jazz embodies all music genres, from blues to standards to everything in between.

Being with Herman gave me an appreciation for all types of music. Watching him interact with students in the classroom made me more excited about my plans to study mass communications at UTC the next year. I chose UTC because one of Herman's friends was the dean of students there and had already promised to get me in for a fraction of the cost.

Ironically it was the same school where my friend Knox had just completed his first summer semester. Knox and I kept our promise to stay in touch through phone calls and letters.

But as fate would have it, Knox had friends in Memphis that he was visiting between the summer and fall semester.

That meant we got to spend a little time together. He and I shared an emotional bond that ran deeper than any ocean. We loved the same types of music, clothes, movies and food. We even loved taking long walks under the stars talking about what our future would be like when I arrived at UTC.

At that point in my life I had gone out on many dates with guys and girls, but I'd never felt for any of them what I felt for Knox. From the way he smelled to the way he kissed to the way he laughed. And even though we never went all the way, I remember feeling his heart beating next to mine.

Knox was in town for a week, but I didn't introduce him to Mom. I guess I wasn't ready to tell her that I was in love with a man for fear of disappointing her or being rejected. The week after Knox headed back home to Nashville, Mom and I started shopping for supplies and clothes for the new school year.

We even looked at things I could possibly use in my college dorm room the next year. Mom was super hyped about me going to college. For years she had been saying, "Go to school while I can help you. Make something of yourself so you can get a good job and make your mama proud."

And she'd say, "Lord knows I don't want you to have to struggle like I did."

I stayed pretty busy my senior year at Hamilton, and I must have missed the clues.

But right after I graduated, Mom suddenly decided she was going to leave Herman and return to Birmingham.

This all happened so fast that it caught me by surprise. I knew the problems they had in the past, but Herman seemed to be thinking more clearly now. Of course, he was still drinking, but he had mellowed tremendously. One night Mom dropped a bomb on me that I never saw coming.

She took me to dinner at my favorite eatery, Captain Bilbo's

River Restaurant. They always had a great band and the shrimp and grits were scrumptious. From any window in the restaurant you could see the "M"-shaped bridge that crossed the Mississippi River and connected Memphis, Tennessee, with West Memphis, Arkansas. I knew it was something serious that Mom wanted to tell me because of that peculiar look on her face. Plus, she reached out and held my hand, which is something she usually reserved for when she really wanted to be heard. That's when she said, "Baby, you know I love you, right?"

"Yes, Mama, I love you more."

Then she said, "But I really need you to do me a very big favor."

"Sure, Mama, I'll do anything for you."

"Baby, I need you to go stay at our house in Birmingham and go to UAB (the University of Alabama at Birmingham) this semester," she said.

My heart started racing and I asked, "Why, Mama?"

Aunt Jean and Granddaddy had been staying in our house since Mom moved to Memphis nearly 10 years earlier. But when Mom told Aunt Jean she was preparing to leave Herman and move back to Birmingham, Aunt Jean went ahead and found them another place to live.

Mom said, "If you will just stay until I can get my ducks in a row, I promise you I'll be home soon and you can go to UTC next year." I was disappointed to say the least, but at the same time I was somewhat excited. If I did as she asked, I'd be in my own place at just 18 years old.

*My grandparents,
James Sylvester and
Mary Emma Childrey*

*Me and Aunt Jean
before the fire*

Christmas Morning at age 5

Me in my favorite shirt

Aunt Jean and Uncle Sonny

Uncle Sonny during the Vietnam War

*Uncle James and
Aunt Yvonne*

*Mom's
Graduation
Picture from
Hayes High
School*

Terri, Andrea, Tonya, and Me

Mom and Herman

Me with my journal

*Mom at
one of
our many
family
BBQs*

Card Party at Mom's Friend House

Deirdre, Edwin, James Jr. and Me

Herman playing with BB King's band

Mom in New York City in 1975 during our first family vacation

NINE

BACK TO BIRMINGHAM

I WAS FRESH out of high school in the summer of 1981 and basically on my own.

The O'Jays were preparing to release their hit single, "Your Body's Here with Me (But Your Mind's on the Other Side of Town)."

And that's exactly how I felt.

Although I was attending UAB, I really wanted to be at UTC studying mass communications with my friend Knox. Instead, I was attending a school that I felt completely detached from. I was alone with no one to answer to and school went downhill fast. It got to the point that I began skipping class almost every week. When I should have been at home studying, I was hanging out at the clubs with my friends drinking and smoking weed. Partying became such a habit that I dropped out of school and got a job working at Century Plaza Mall again, this time for JC Penney.

My cousin Cheryl and I both applied for the sales position, but they didn't hire her. I guess they hired me because I had the experience of working for Kinney Shoes. Plus, I had worked at Goldsmith's Department Store during the summer breaks when I'd visit Mom in Memphis. Even though I started as a JCP sales associate, I quickly worked my way into a supervisor role. I've always been the creative type, and I found myself remerchandising the whole men's department.

The store manager noticed my skills and offered me a job working with the visual merchandising team. That eventually led to me becoming the department's supervisor.

On my lunch breaks I'd walk out into the mall to check out other store windows or to just people watch. One particular day I walked into a small men's store called Jeans West. It was the kind of store that sold trendy clothes and played loud music. The manager was a handsome, dark-skinned guy with a thick mustache and a personality that made you feel comfortable to be around.

His name was Chazz and our relationship developed to the point that I would spend my entire lunch break in his store talking about church, choirs and fashion. We both had a passion for all of those things.

The day Chazz said, "I love Ebony Fashion Fair," my heart skipped a couple of beats.

I had seen the Ebony Fashion Fair fashion show the year before at the Boutwell Auditorium with my cousins Delois and Cheryl. Delois was a member of Delta Sigma Theta Sorority. Every year they would sponsor the show as a charity event. I told Chazz, "I love Shayla Simpson," the show's commentator. She spoke in a slow, methodical rhythm that was seductive and captivating. He laughed and said, "I love her too."

"In fact, I've always had dreams of being the male version of Shayla Simpson," I said.

"Really? Let me hear you." So I gave him a little taste of what I could do, and he loved it.

That year he asked me to commentate his store's fashion show at the mall's spring event. The show was in the center of the mall with bright lights, lots of theatrics, high-energy music and hundreds of people watching and listening. That was the first time I had ever performed in front of so many people. And even though my knees were shaking and I could feel my heart racing, no one in the audience was the wiser.

The show was a huge success. In fact, after that, I even started commentating shows for Penney's.

Chazz went on to start his own traveling fashion show called, *The Chazz Fashion Review*. He asked me to be the commentator and to record a promotional spot. We recorded the commercial downtown at WENN, the most-listened to black-owned radio station in Birmingham. After hearing the commercial, station manager Dave Donnell offered me a job on the spot. He was a radio icon in Birmingham.

At the time I was only 20 years old and full of potential waiting to be tapped into. When this opportunity came along I was thrilled, but deep inside, I knew it was not the job for me. Being a DJ never really appealed to me.

But I was not about to turn down the opportunity to at least get my leg in the door. I had hoped to eventually become the big voice that you hear advertising the station throughout the day. I had never done radio before, but Dave asked me to come down and observe the guys that were already working there. I had sat in on about two sessions before that Saturday morning when my phone rang.

The voice on the other end was Dave Donnell. He said, "Well, buddy, are you about ready to go on the air?"

My heart fluttered, but I said, "Yes, I'm ready."

"If you will come down about 4:30 we'll get set up," he said.

When I got there, the station's hottest DJ, Tyrone Robinson, was on the air. So I thought I would get to sit with him and he'd guide me along, letting me talk on the mic while he watched and gave instructions.

But that's not at all what happened.

After Tyrone put on the next record he turned to me and said, "Man, thank you so much, I really appreciate you sitting in for me because I have something I have to do."

Tyrone then took off his headphones, shook my hand and in "Elvis" style, left the building. Dave turned to me and said, "Take the wheel, Captain."

He added, "If you don't do anything else, please make sure you keep the music playing. Remember to give the weather and the time and you'll be all right. OK, I'll be listening in just in case anything should happen."

He then took out a card, scribbled his number on it and said, "Here, call me if you need me." That's when he went the way of Tyrone, and I was all alone in the most popular soul radio station in Birmingham.

In the softly lit studio all I could see were buttons, music carts and a microphone. Then before I knew it, my time had come.

"Hello, Birmingham, I'm Lawayne Childrey. I'll be rocking the mic for Tyrone Robinson until 10 tonight. I hope you'll sit back, relax and enjoy the ride."

My heart was racing a mile a minute, but I was actually on the air. I was living a dream that thousands of people wished they could experience in real life. During the next few hours my adrenaline was off the charts. Even if I didn't do that much talking I was actually doing my first radio show, but the truth is, I wasn't loving it.

I felt like I was thrown into a pool filled with sharks and that I was doomed to die. But I survived and actually did a pretty good job. Not only did I keep the show moving with having only a minimal amount of training, I was proud of the work. However, I called Dave the next day and thanked him for the opportunity but said I didn't think I was cut out to be a DJ. Even though I may have had the voice, it just wasn't what I wanted to do at the time.

Chazz's traveling fashion show went on to become a notable success, and we spent a lot of time together. The show wooed crowds in Atlanta, Memphis, Nashville, and, of course, Birmingham. I still remember the cool, slow, masculine walk I'd take to my stool where I sat to commentate. It was all done over the smooth sounds of soft jazz, Latin and R&B.

"Welcome to the Chazz Fashion Review. It's more than just a fashion show. It's a show featuring some of America's newest and hottest designers."

On cue, the models would take the runway, strutting the hottest fashion looks of the day.

It was after the final curtain call one night in Birmingham that I realized I had unexpectedly fallen in love. Chazz, a man 12 years older than I and just divorced, was suddenly my everything, and I was his.

TEN

CAN'T HIDE LOVE

ONE PHONE CALL can change everything.

Even though Mom was still in Memphis, she stayed in constant contact with me. I could count on us talking almost every night and what seemed like all day on the weekends. But nearly every time she called I had company, and it was always a guy. None of them were romantic interests, just friends.

This particular Sunday afternoon my friend Ray and I were sitting in the living room, smoking weed and listening to music. The sound of us singing along to Jennifer Holiday's "And I am Telling You" was cut short.

Ring! Ring! Ring!

Ray shouted out, "Oh no, not the phone—just when it's getting to the good part."

I said, "Hold on, let me get it. Hello."

The voice on the other end said, "Hi, baby."

I said, "Hi, Mom."

That's when Ray took a pull off of the joint so hard that it made him cough. Mom heard him and asked, "Do you have company?"

I said, "Yes, it's my friend Ray."

"Ray? Have I met him?"

"No, ma'am, but you'll have to meet him when you come home; he's really funny."

Then out of the blue she asked, "Are you gay?"

There was an awkward moment of silence before I rhetorically asked, "Am I gay?"

"Yes. Are you gay?"

My jaw dropped, eyes bucked and my heart fluttered. I put my hand over the receiver and mouthed to Ray, "My mom just asked me if I'm gay."

With a look of surprise on his face he mouthed back. "What? Oh my God!"

I then took a deep breath and squeaked out a nervous laugh. After a long exhale I was finally able to speak.

"Mom, why would you ask me something like that?"

"Because I want to know," she said.

I started getting really nervous because I knew she was serious.

There was a long pause between us.

Even though Jennifer Holiday was still playing in the background you could hear a pin drop in the room.

Then I asked again, "Am I gay?"

"Yes, son, are you gay?"

Mom and I never kept secrets from each other. I always felt like I could tell her anything. But this is the one secret I had kept to myself. As long as I could remember, Mom always told me, "Just let me know what's going on and I'll know how to deal with it."

So after a giant sigh and a big swallow I said, "Yes, ma'am, I am gay."

As soon as I got it out Mom was saying, "I thought so." She then went on to ask, "How long have you and Ray been dating?"

That question brought me back to reality.

"Mom, Ray is not my lover, he's my friend."

She asked in a surprised voice, "Your friend?"

"Yes, ma'am, my friend."

Mom has always been very direct, so it didn't surprise me to hear the next words that came out of her mouth.

"Well, do you have a lover?"

I said, "Yes. My lover's name is Chazz."

Before Mom even asked anything about Chazz she was asking, "How long have you been gay?"

While I was still nervous, I was relieved the lie that I had felt forced to live with was finally out in the open. At last I was beginning to embrace my truth.

So I answered her question. "I think I've been gay all my life."

Then she asked, "Was it something I did to make you gay?"

"No, Mom, even though I've dated girls, I've always been attracted to guys."

The next question surprised me. "Would you like to talk to somebody?"

I asked, "Talk to somebody?"

"Yes, maybe a therapist or someone?" she explained.

"No, Mom, I don't think there is anything wrong with me."

That's when the big question came.

"Does this mean that I won't ever have any grandchildren?"

That question caught me off guard and I had to clear my throat again before I could say anything.

"Mom, I can't answer that because I really don't know what the future holds."

I was relieved that the conversation had finally come up, but I was also afraid of disappointing her because, as an only child, I knew I was her only hope of having grandchildren.

Then I asked, "Mom, are you mad at me?"

"Am I mad at you?" she asked. "Why would I be mad at you?"

"Because I'm gay," I said.

"No, I'm not mad at you. You're my son, I'll love you no matter if you're gay, straight, blue or green."

She went on to ask, "But how do you know you are gay?"

I told her, "Mom, it's just something I know and have known for years."

From that point she wanted to know about this friend and that friend and this girl and this guy, and the questions went on and on and on.

Finally, she must have run out of things to ask and she said, in a very stern voice, "Well, I'll tell you what, I don't like it!"

Then her tone softened as she said, "But you're my son and I only want what's best for you and what makes you happy. Plus, I don't want to lose you."

At last I had freed myself from one of the biggest secrets that I had carried for years. "Mom, you said you thought I was gay. How?"

"Son, a mother knows her child."

But she said what really fueled her suspicion was a letter from Knox that I had left out on my bed in Memphis. She said after reading the love letter she asked Herman's friend at UTC about him. Mom said he told her Knox was a nice enough kid, but he hung with a pretty gay group of friends.

She told me that was the reason she didn't want me to go to UTC, but that she was sorry and only wanted me to be happy.

"Who else in our family knows you're gay?"

I told her it's never been an issue that I discuss because I never wanted to be labeled as the gay guy. I told her I only want to be known as the guy who is smart, talented and loves his mom.

"Son, I love you too," she said. "I'll always love you, but I want to meet this guy, Chazz."

"Sure, Mom, you will meet him as soon as you get home."

I wanted Mom to meet Chazz and see us together. In fact, I needed that because I wanted her to know that even though I was gay, I was still the same son she had raised and was proud of.

Mom and Chazz hit it off instantly. But that didn't stop her from interrogating him. Just as their visit was ending, Mom reached out and embraced Chazz's hands in hers. She looked him squarely in his eyes and said, "You be good to my son. And remember, if you fuck over him you will have to deal with me."

I remember laughter filling the air as Mom and Chazz hugged. She and I also embraced before she got into her car and drove to Aunt Jean's house for dinner.

From that point on, whenever Mom would come home to visit I'd always make sure that we all did something special together, like go to a concert or out to dinner with my aunt and a few cousins. I wanted them all to see that even though I was involved with a man, I was the same Lawayne that they knew.

ELEVEN

LOVE HURTS

"LET HIM WHO is without sin cast the first stone."

That is perhaps one of the most well-known lessons of the Bible. It's also a lesson that I had to learn the hard way. About 6 months into my relationship with Chazz, I discovered a serious character flaw about myself. It's something I never noticed until it literally hit me square in the face.

One night while he was visiting me at home, some other friends came over. It was cold that night, and I remember telling my friends Michael and Keith to put their coats in my bedroom. Michael took Keith's coat and flipped on the light switch behind the mirror on my dresser. It was a very inconspicuous spot. He laid the coats on my bed, flipped the light back off and came into the den.

We were all sitting around listening to music, sipping gin and juice and talking about our favorite movies.

When I went into the kitchen to freshen everyone's drinks, Chazz followed me. While standing at the counter he grabbed me from behind and wrapped his arms around my waist. He squeezed me a lot tighter than he usually did.

Then he kissed the back of my neck and whispered in my ear, "How did he know where your light switch was?"

I turned around and looked him in the face and asked, "Huh?"

He said, "We'll talk about it later."

The rest of the night was uncomfortable, to say the least. I couldn't help but wonder what Chazz was talking about. When Michael and Keith left I put on my denim jacket and grabbed my car keys off the dresser. I had to drive Chazz to his apartment because he had been riding with me all day. As soon as we got into my beige Nissan Maxima, he started yelling.

"What the fuck was that about?"

I had never seen that sort of wildness in his eyes before.

He asked, "Are you sleeping with him?"

"Sleeping with who?" I asked.

"Michael," he said. "Are you sleeping with him?"

The truth is, I was only 20 years old. Plus, I was young, dumb and full of stupidity. Yes, I was sleeping with Chazz, Michael and probably a couple of other guys. When I admitted that to Chazz, he hauled off and gave me a backhanded slap. It turned my face black and blue and made my ears ring for what seemed like hours.

As stupid as I had been, I still wasn't going to take that abuse. So I told him we were through. He immediately started sobbing uncontrollably and said, "Baby, I'm so sorry, please forgive me. I don't know what came over me. It's just that I love you so much I can't stand the thought of you being with someone else."

For the rest of that 5-minute ride my heart was galloping. I took several deep breaths to relieve the pressure that was building up inside. Still I remained silent and in shock from the violence that had just been inflicted upon me. It took me back to the days when Mom use to get beaten down by Dex. So much rage had built up inside of me that when we arrived at his house I parked the car and slapped him even harder than he had slapped me.

That's when I told Chazz to "Get the fuck out of my car and never call me again." Crying and holding his face he apologized again saying, "Baby, please forgive me. I am so sorry; I never meant to hit you."

As soon as he got out and closed the door I sped away and swore never to see him again. Although I was exhausted from the fight, I found it hard to fall asleep that night. How could I allow myself to become so enraged that I would actually want to fight someone? I had only been in one fight in my life and that was with a guy in elementary school. He was just a big bully who liked to pick on everyone.

This was not me.

I spent most of the night playing the whole scene over and over in my head. After about 3 hours of sleep I was awakened by the doorbell. My gut instinct told me it was Chazz, and I didn't know if I should answer it. But when I got to the door it was a deliveryman from Contri Brothers' flower and catering shop. He had a huge basket wrapped in red cellophane with a big red bow and streamers.

When I signed for that basket, I was accepting much more than flowers. Over the next 12 years, Chazz and I danced together, traveled together and made love together. But we also cheated on each other. And whenever we would catch each other misbehaving, it would always erupt into a jealous rage followed by more blind passion.

Yet our worlds were so intertwined I feared that only death could tear us apart. At least I knew it was unhealthy to live that way and because of the volatility of our relationship I started leaning more toward my family.

One of the people that I confided in was my cousin Cheryl. She was a beautiful chocolate-brown girl with a smile and dimples that could light up the world. Cheryl was 2 years older than I and we basically grew up together. Our moms were first cousins and best friends, so we spent a lot of time together. When we were little kids we used to shoot marbles, make mud cakes and walk to her granddad's store to beg for candy treats.

As we grew older we remained friends, talking on the phone and visiting each other every chance we got. As the seasons changed we remained close but found new interests in life.

She found James, and I found Chazz.

I never knew a lot about James, but I do know he was the love of her life. They did everything together.

After Cheryl and James married, they moved to Atlanta and seemed to have a fabulous life. She had a good job with Xerox, and he was a building contractor. They didn't have any children together, but she had a love child from her teen years. James and Cheryl had been trying to start a family, but it just wasn't working out. In the meantime, Cheryl began getting sick and the doctors were dumbfounded.

They ran tests for this and tests for that. They poked, prodded and scanned everything but couldn't find anything to explain her illness. Being a close-knit family we all were greatly concerned with what was going on with her.

After utilizing nearly every test imaginable one of the

dozens of doctors treating Cheryl decided to test her for HIV. During that time, HIV/AIDS was considered to be a gay male disease. Seldom did you hear of women getting it. Unfortunately, not only did the test come back positive for HIV, it also showed that the virus had developed into full-blown AIDS

We were all shocked.

I asked myself, "How could this very straight, young, beautiful black woman who was only beginning to enjoy life have AIDS?"

Family whispers had it that her husband was an intravenous drug user and that she had contracted it from him. The diagnosis caused so much pain and discord in my family that it left Cheryl broken in ways I could only imagine.

As she began receiving treatment to fight the disease her company announced they were downsizing. They gave her the option of relocating to Tampa, Florida, or lose her job. Reluctantly, Cheryl chose to move to Tampa. However, she really didn't have much of a choice. She needed her health insurance to pay for the mountain of medical and prescription bills that were piling up.

Let's face it, back then in the early '90s there weren't many medications developed to fight AIDS, and those that were available were so expensive that the average person couldn't possibly afford them even with insurance. It was common for HIV/AIDS medications to cost thousands of dollars per month for just *one* prescription.

By keeping her job, Cheryl at least had access to insurance to help pay for her medicines she had to take. Unfortunately, living in Tampa she didn't have the hands-on support that she needed from her family and friends. Any doctor would agree that family support is vitally important for anyone going through a life-altering situation, especially something as devastating as AIDS.

Cheryl was miserable in Tampa, but she continued to stay there until her body had given out and she could no longer work. She eventually moved back to Birmingham and spent her final days surrounded by the love and care of her brothers, sister and other family members, including myself.

When I first found out Cheryl had AIDS it tripped me out completely. How does an intelligent young woman with a squeaky-clean image come down with AIDS? I'm almost certain my cousin couldn't have been half as promiscuous as I had been. At that time I was a 20-something-year-old with raging hormones who wanted to have it all.

But when Cheryl tested positive it gave me a reality check. So I went to the public health department to receive a free HIV test. However, doing so was not an easy task. I was afraid for so many reasons. One was that the test might come back positive, I'd end up sick and eventually die way too young just like I'd seen dozens of my friends do.

Another reason it was so difficult for me to go get tested was because I just didn't want anyone to see me going to the health department, or the "free clinic," as so many people called it.

You see, in 1991, the stigma associated with HIV and AIDS was even stronger than it is today. Nobody in the gay community wanted to be seen near a health department because of the ridicule they would encounter.

The stigma was so bad that my first thought was to park my car blocks away and walk to the testing clinic. Then I began thinking someone would surely see me walking into the clinic and put the pieces together. So I decided to park my car in the parking deck. Even then, I was afraid I'd know the parking attendant or someone else and I'd have to explain why I was there.

Then after I made it into the building there was the daunting task of asking someone to direct me to the infectious disease clinic.

My stomach was in knots.

Finally, I made it into the clinic and told the receptionist, "I'm here to take a free HIV test."

At that time you could test anonymously. So I gave them a fictitious name that they matched with a corresponding number.

As I was sitting in the waiting room, I noticed that the other people who were also waiting to be seen by the doctor or to be tested seemed relaxed. They were laughing and talking, watching TV and flipping through magazines. That helped me relax some and take my mind off of the fact that I was about to take a test that could determine the rest of my life.

Finally, my number was called, and I was escorted into a small room where I received a short briefing on how the virus is contracted. I was also counseled on why it's important to be tested and the importance of practicing safe sex.

As they stuck the needle in my vein to draw the vials of blood, I sat there cool as a cucumber on the outside, but it felt like I was dying on the inside. Somehow, I knew that if my young beautiful, talented, well educated and very straight female cousin could have AIDS, surly my chances of having the virus were astronomical. Besides, I knew Cheryl couldn't have been half as reckless as I had been.

Finally after about 20 minutes passed, the nurse, along with a doctor, came back into the room and told me exactly what I had feared. *"You have come into contact with HIV, the virus that causes AIDS."*

I didn't flinch. I didn't cry. All I could do was sit there in silence with my whole sexual life flashing before my eyes. I couldn't help thinking about all the stupid things I'd done, like not wearing a condom and sleeping with multiple partners. All of those images flashed before my eyes.

Nearly everyone knows the song by TLC called "Waterfalls." In the song the group says, "I know that you're going to have it your way or nothing at all but I think you're moving too fast."

At just 25 years old, I knew I had been moving way too fast for the past 10 years. So there I was, sitting in silence that felt like a bad dream I couldn't wake up from.

That's when the doctor asked, "Did you hear me? You have HIV."

I said yes. I could tell they were surprised by my reaction . . . or lack of emotion to their words, but I kept saying to myself, "I'm going to beat this thing."

Again they asked, "Did you hear me? You have come into contact with the virus that causes AIDS."

All I could do was say, "Yes."

I couldn't cry.

I couldn't scream.

I couldn't even get angry.

All I could do was breathe.

I didn't know it at the time, but I was actually in deep denial. Without even realizing it I was attempting to calm my anxiety by denying the facts. I think the doctor was more than a little concerned about how calm I was about the test results and what it meant.

But the truth is, I guess I felt that the diagnosis was punishment I deserved.

The doctor told me that even though I tested positive they still wanted me to see an HIV specialist to confirm the test and see how much damage had been done to my body. They suggested the 1917 Clinic at UAB, which specializes in HIV treatment and research. But because of the harsh stigma I did not want to run the risk of seeing anyone I knew going into the clinic. So the doctor gave me a list of private physicians who were accepting HIV-positive patients. They also gave me the name of some AIDS service organizations that could offer me free counseling, medication and other assistance.

But before I left the clinic that day the doctor, social worker, or nurse, I don't remember exactly which one, asked me to give the names of the people I had slept with recently.

Of course, I hesitated because who wants to have to share that kind of information with a stranger? And even though I was to give them their names, I also knew I needed to tell them myself. I figured it would be best to hear something so serious coming from me. However, the first person I told was not anyone I slept with. The first person I told was my darling mother. By that time I had heard horror stories from friends whose parents had put them put of their house after finding out they were HIV positive—all because they were afraid they would catch it from a toilet seat or eating out of the same dish or drinking out of a glass they had used, even though they all had been washed and sanitized with bleach . . . They were still afraid of contracting the virus.

My darling mother was always so cool and so comforting. She was deeply saddened by the dreadful news. However, in her own ever-endearing way, she assured me that God would work it out for me.

"Baby, I love you," she said. "And I'm confident that with all the new medicines out you're going to be just fine."

Glory be to God, my mother was right. I was going to be OK because the doctors had detected the virus in my body early. It hadn't multiplied to the point where it had caused any major damage to my blood cells. That meant I was still nearly as healthy as the average person.

I did find a doctor who specialized in HIV to monitor the progression of the disease in my body. They even started me on AZT, which was one of the few medications available in the early 1990s. After 3 months, my doctor determined the drug wasn't helping me, but it wasn't hurting me either. But because it was so toxic we decided it would be best for me to come off of AZT, or any meds, until the virus had started increasing.

That first night after I found out, I told my lover Chazz that I tested HIV positive. I didn't know what his reaction would be because we had seen dozens of our friends fall victim to the disease. Luckily for me, he was very supportive. Chazz told me that he would always be there for me and that it didn't matter what I had, he would always love me just the same. He also said he went to be tested in his private doctor's office the next day.

He said the results came back negative, but I never really believed him. Red flags were flying because even though I tried to introduce condoms into our relationship, he insisted that it was still OK for us to have unprotected sex.

I knew it was wrong, but I still trusted him.

Remember I said I was young, dumb and full of stupidity?

Allow me to add naive to that list. I was 25 years old and in love with a man 12 years older than I.

I understood the importance of protecting others. But I was still putting myself at risk. I didn't fully understand the importance of protecting myself from other strands of the virus or other sexually transmitted diseases. Six months later, Chazz said he retested and his results were still negative. I started feeling better about his health and mine, so I stopped bugging him so much about us using condoms.

Obviously, we were both in denial.

Years passed, and as we continued our reckless lovemaking he always insisted that his status remained negative.

Even though Chazz and I had a multitude of problems, we managed to stay together for more than a decade. Sometimes things got so bad that we literally fought like cats and dogs because he was unfaithful and so was I. I can't count the number of affairs we had on each other, how many fights we had or how many times we made up. The relationship was so volatile that our bodies would often end up with cuts, scrapes and bruises that had to be explained to family and friends.

In addition to our bodies being torn to shreds, our homes would also often end up in ruins.

Pictures were torn from the walls, and lamps were thrown across the room. I even slammed my Maxima into his Mercedes in a state of rage. The scene was so dark that either of us could have ended up dead from the fights that spurred from jealousy.

Even though the police were called numerous times, neither of us was ever arrested. I didn't have the strength to leave Chazz because I had developed a codependency toward him. I had reached a place where I felt like I needed to be with Chazz in order to be complete. I suffered from low self-esteem and didn't think anyone else would love me because of my HIV status.

Whenever I threatened to leave, Chazz would always say I was going to need him to take care of me when I got down sick from AIDS. He would often tell me that if I left him, he would tell everyone at my church and my job that I had AIDS.

I was terrorized.

I was tired of the fights and the lies and the infidelity, but I stayed. I had fallen victim to the same drama that we see in so many relationships, be it straight or gay.

As the years passed, Chazz continued to tell me that he was HIV negative. But ironically, as I remained strong and healthy, he became frail and sickly. Chazz had developed a bad cold that he called a sinus infection. Then he began breaking out into hives and shingles, eventually ending up in the hospital a couple of times.

By that time, he and his ex-wife had long been divorced. But because I was considered by doctors as only a friend, I never really knew exactly what was going on with him.

Chazz was such a secretive person that I don't think he actually told anyone in his family that he was sick. I think it was part of his Southern upbringing not to ever air his dirty laundry.

Even when your loved one is lying on their deathbed eaten up with cancer, diabetes or even complications from AIDS, it's customary to tell everyone that they are fine. In the South, we learned quickly not to put our business in the street. However, Chazz and I did have the love and support of my family.

Mom had moved back to Birmingham to open and manage a communications company. It was the same company she had worked for part time in Memphis. She, along with Aunt Jean and my cousin Delois, would take turns stopping by our house on their lunch breaks. They made sure that Chazz and the house were clean and that he had a hot meal to eat, even if he couldn't keep it down.

One day when I came home from work he asked me a troubling question. "Did you see the nurse?"

I quickly replied, "No! What nurse?"

He said, "Oh, my doctor wants me to have breathing

treatments, so they are sending a nurse out to see me. She just left."

That's when I knew Chazz was sicker than any of us really knew. A week later, he ended up in the hospital with pneumonia.

A light-skinned, heavy-hipped nurse that stood about 5 feet 6 inches tall saw me every day. She knew I was at his side nearly around the clock, only taking breaks to go to work. I'd even come by on my lunch break to check in on him.

This particular day as I was walking to Chazz's room she grabbed my hand and pulled me aside. I can still remember her long wavy, jet-black hair and the beautiful smile on her face. But what I remember most is the way she held my hands in hers. The way she rubbed them gently as if to prepare me for some unsettling news. While cupping my hands in hers, she stared directly into my eyes and said in a stern yet gentle voice, "Take good care of him, baby, he is really sick."

After she spoke, I couldn't say a word. I shed a tear, took my hands out of hers and wrapped my arms around her shoulders to whisper in her ear. All I could say was, "Thank you so much, I will."

I continued the walk to Chazz's room where I stopped at the door. I had to put on one of the yellow paper gowns and masks that everyone was required to wear. Chazz was lying in bed. His gray gown with blue polka dots was loosely tied at the neck, and his right shoulder was exposed. I fixed his gown, pulled his white sheets and the two green cotton blankets up over his shoulders to keep him warm. I also fluffed his pillows, trying to make him a little more comfortable.

After giving him a hug and a kiss, I pulled one of the two wood-framed chairs up to his bed and sat there rubbing his legs through the blankets. I knew he was nauseated and in pain, but I still asked him how he was feeling. He said, "I feel OK, I guess, but I've been better."

"I know it's hard right now," I said. "But things will get better, you just wait and see. I've got you all the way."

I was still avoiding the truth, still naive.

He tried to smile, but at that point even smiling was painful for Chazz. I tried to engage him in small chitchat just to let him know that I was there, but he wanted to talk about something deeper.

He said, "There is something I need to tell you."

Even though I didn't know what he wanted to say, my heart began to flutter.

That's when he pulled his left hand from under the cover, reaching for me. I held his hand and rubbed it gently. He then told me, "They tested me for HIV today."

"Oh, OK," I said. "How did it come out?"

"They say I'm HIV positive."

Without even as much as a sigh or a pause, I said, "It's OK. We'll get through this too."

Of course this was not shocking news to me. In fact, it was somewhat of a relief.

No, I was not happy to hear Chazz say he was HIV positive. However, I was glad to know that he was finally trying to deal with his denial. The truth of the matter is that by then, Chazz was so eaten up with the disease that an incurable fungus had attacked most of his body, including his brain.

He was so heavily sedated that he was only able to stay awake for short periods of time. Later that morning, Chazz took a turn for the worse. His doctors called in his loved ones to give us all the news.

Besides my family, he only had a couple of his family members coming to check on him. I think he wanted it that way because even with the hundreds of friends and acquaintances he had, most people didn't understand HIV/AIDS.

In the early '90s, many people were afraid to even be in the presence of someone with the disease. That's why I think he never let his family know exactly how sick he was. The doctors told us they had done all they could do for Chazz. They said it was just a matter of time, maybe days—or even hours—before he would succumb to complications of the disease.

I had to get away.

I felt like I wanted to scream. Even though we had fought like enemies, I still felt like I was losing my best friend, partner and lifeline.

When his sisters got to the hospital, only one of them went into Chazz's room to spend time with him. The other sat in the waiting room because she said, "I can't stand seeing him in that condition."

Ironically, she was the one he thought he could depend on if anything ever happened to him. He had even made her the executor of his estate. But even as he was fighting for his last breath, she couldn't find the strength to comfort him.

I knew things were quickly deteriorating for Chazz. But I thought since his sisters were there I'd have a chance to just get away to exhale and talk to God about everything that was happening.

When I left the hospital, I was feeling really sad. It was like the world was coming to a standstill because everything was beginning to move in slow motion. I wanted to eat something, but I didn't have an appetite. I wanted to go talk to Mom or a friend, but everybody was at work.

I ended up going to a music store in the mall where I purchased the new CD by Andraé Crouch called *Mercy*. When

I got to the car I tore the plastic off, popped the CD in and listened to them sing.

"In times like these, Mercy is what we need. Oh, Lord, Oh, Lord, won't you have Mercy please."

Those words echoed in my head over and over again.

"In times like these, Mercy is what we need. Oh, Lord, Oh, Lord, won't you have Mercy please."

I must have listened to the whole CD once before I made my way back to the hospital. Just as I was pulling into the parking lot, my cell phone rang. It was Chazz's sister telling me he had just died. I parked the car and walked into the hospital. But the only thing I could focus on were the words in the song.

"In times like these, Mercy is what we need. Oh, Lord, Oh, Lord, won't you have Mercy please."

When I stepped out of the elevator, I scurried down the hall and into his room. His sisters were gathered around the bed, but all I could focus on was the man lying there.

By then, the nurses had taken the tubes out of him and for the first time in months he looked like he was at peace. There was no more labored breathing, no coughing, no sweating, no more chills or tears. Finally, God had taken Chazz home where he could have perfect rest.

To say I was crushed would be an understatement. Even though Chazz and I had our problems over the years, I still loved him dearly.

That week, his family asked me to help organize his funeral. I picked out the wooden mahogany casket, selected a cream-colored suit and coordinated it with the perfect tie. The coffin was draped in a blanket of cream-colored roses.

The week culminated in a beautiful home going celebration befitting a man who loved life, people and above all else, God.

Even though Chazz and I were together for years, it took his death to teach me what true commitment means. Yes, we had our share of ups and downs, but we were still a team. We invested in each other on every level.

However, when he got sick, and especially when he died, I found myself at the mercy of his family. Although we were together more than a decade, I had no legal rights to his affairs.

That meant I didn't have legal access to his bank account, our home, our automobiles or any of the personal possessions that we had collected together. Even though I never asked his family for a dime, it was degrading to watch them come in and claim whatever they wanted.

His sister even told me if he wanted me to have it he would have put my name on it. After what seemed like a lifetime of committing to this man, I was even denied information concerning his medical care.

Chazz died on Tuesday morning. We buried him Saturday afternoon.

After the funeral, burial and repast, I went back to the cemetery and said my final good-byes. Standing atop the fresh layer of red dirt on his grave, I became filled with emotion and began to sob.

My mind quickly went back to the first time I met the 5 foot 9-inch chocolate drop of a man with the thick mustache. He was handsome, suave and debonair. He also had a heart of gold and spoiled me rotten. I thanked him for every good thing that I could remember about him.

I said, "Thank you for loving me unconditionally, and for allowing me to love you back. Thanks for allowing me to showcase my talents in your fashion show. And thanks for the music box you gave me with the card that said, 'I am your biggest fan and I know this music box will be the first of many more trophies to come.'"

As I kneeled there sobbing and throwing rose petals on the newly filled grave, my emotions changed to anger.

"How dare you die on me," I said. "How dare you lie and say you were negative when you knew all along you were positive."

Even in death, our relationship went from one extreme to the other.

At that point I fell to my knees and hands like a dog and cried hysterically. After a while I wiped the tears from my eyes, brushed the red clay dirt from my hands and knees and I told Chazz good-bye. "I love you, and I'll always miss you. Good night, sweet prince."

TWELVE

WHAT'S THIS WORD CALLED LOVE?

ON MONDAY MORNING I began packing up our apartment. The memories were just too hard to bear.

I could have moved back home with Mom, but I knew that would be a temporary situation. So I found a cool brownstone in the heart of Five Points South. It was called the Drake, and it was located in a trendy section of Birmingham.

The apartment was great. It had beautiful hardwood floors. The floor-to-ceiling windows along with the black-and-white tiles in the kitchen gave the place a warm energy that drew me in. The sun-filled kitchen had a dazzling view of the downtown Birmingham skyline. From the bedroom I could see and hear the dancing fountain that sat in front of the cosmetic surgery center behind the Drake. And from any room there was a bird's-eye view of Vulcan, the giant cast-iron statue of the Roman God of Fire that stands atop Red Mountain overlooking the city.

Five Points is the type of community where you can walk out of your door and be at the local grocery store, a fine restaurant or a swanky little jazz club within 2 minutes. It's one of the few neighborhoods in the city where the very rich lived right next door to the very poor. There was always something interesting to look at in Five Points, like the gay pride parade or the muscle car show or shirtless men shooting hoops down at UAB. In other words, Five Points was the perfect spot for any gay man living in Birmingham.

I'd been settled in my apartment about 6 months. Even though I was spending lots of time with family and friends, things weren't the same without Chazz. I was not only grief stricken but bored and very lonely. So I started hanging out at the clubs trying to meet someone I could depend on for nighttime company. One night on the way home I met a guy who was also leaving the club.

We pulled up to the red light at the same time. He looked at me. I looked at him. It was like I was gazing at an angel. He was jet black, muscular, flashed a wide bright smile and there was a soft white glow that hovered over his head like a halo. His name was Chico. We exchanged numbers, and talked on the phone into the wee hours of the morning. His sense of humor kept me laughing, which made it hard to end the conversation. Before forcing ourselves to hang up, we made plans to have dinner at my place the next night.

Just before Chico got to my apartment, I made sure everything was in place. The salad was chilling, baked potatoes warming and the steaks were tender and juicy. Luther Vandross and Anita Baker were playing in the background. With the blinds wide open, Vulcan Park and the downtown skyline put the finishing touches on a romantic backdrop.

When Chico knocked on the door, my heart skipped a beat.

But I quickly put my game face on and opened the door to the most gorgeous, baldheaded, African prince I had seen in a long time. Chico was 12 years younger than I. He stood about 6 foot 1, weighed 185 pounds and had a muscular frame with a bubble butt as soft as a pillow. I found that out quickly, because when he entered the room I wrapped my arms around his waist, kissed his lips and held him tight. It had been so long since I felt that type of chemistry.

I didn't want to appear desperate, so I stepped back and took a long look at him. He just stood there knowing he was being inspected and met with approval.

I'll never forget the way my arms felt around his tight waist or the way that orange body shirt hugged his physique just tight enough to show every ripple in his abdomen and every pec in his chest right down to the tension in his nipples.

Before dinner we sat in the kitchen getting to know each other better. He said he worked as a laborer, but his true passion was singing. He was a member of his church choir as well as a popular community choir. He even crooned a little bit when one of Luther Vandross's songs made its way into the CD rotation.

As I prepared to serve dinner I was secretly hoping Chico would be dessert.

After the meal we had drinks in my bedroom where we listened to the sounds of the dancing fountains outside my window and gazed up at Vulcan all night from my waterbed. We talked. We kissed. He serenaded me. And we made sweet safe love.

All I really wanted was company, a little "live-in teddy" as I like to call it, someone to hold me tight and whisper sweet nothings in my ear.

What I got was a caring, sensitive man who was incredibly

romantic and would go out of his way to make me happy. I'll never forget the night I came home from work to a surprise picnic in the living room. Chico had decorated the entire apartment with candlelight. Brightly colored tablecloths were laid out on the floor in the middle of the room. It was topped with a centerpiece made of all of my favorite fresh fruits. The grapes, strawberries, kiwi and pineapples tickled my sense of smell the moment I entered the apartment. The sweet aroma of rose petals led to the bathroom where a hot bubble bath awaited me. The bubbles sparkled under the soft glowing candlelight and the sexy sounds of Kenny G whispered in my ears. As I lay soaking in a tub of fragrant bubbles, Chico brought in my favorite cocktail, took a sip and let me taste it on his lips before setting it by the tub.

I finished up my bath and slipped into the black silk boxers and T-shirt he had laid out for me. When I made it into the living room he was wearing only a simple white apron.

He refreshed our drinks and served my favorite meal: a garden salad, loaded baked potato and a juicy rib eye grilled to perfection. For dessert, we fed each other sugary sweet strawberries dipped in freshly whipped cream. That led to making sweet love until we fell asleep in each other's arms.

Before I knew it I was totally submerged in Chico's affection. Even though he was young, he impressed me as being extremely mature, and I knew he was into me.

It's funny how God really does give us what we pray for, and Lord knows I was lonely and praying for that little "live-in teddy." After dating for a couple of months Chico turned out to be that teddy, and more.

Still grieving the death of my lover of more than a decade, I was also vulnerable and my judgment was cloudy. I never meant to fall in love with Chico.

141

In my mind, it didn't matter that things weren't perfect with us. His car was broken down and had been in the repair shop since we began dating. But I didn't mind letting him drive me to work while he drove my car to his job. I didn't care that it was in Pinson, 40 miles north of Birmingham.

But the night I received a call from the police asking if I had given Rico Presley permission to drive my car should have been a wake-up call. I didn't know it at the time, but Chico didn't have a driver's license. So when the cops pulled him over in a routine traffic stop, he gave them his twin brother's name.

So what did I do?

I took him to the department of public safety and got him the books to study for his driver's permit. A few weeks later, Chico was taking the driving test in my car, and he passed. By then, I was beginning to realize that I wasn't in love with someone who was my equal but rather a kid who was raw, uneducated and in need of guidance.

I wanted to love Chico the way I wanted Chazz to love me— to lead me, guide me, protect me and help me to grow into a better man. There was a whole different climate in this relationship, but we made it work.

Chico had been living with me for about 6 months when Mom got a promotion on her job. But the career move also meant she'd have to physically move to Nashville.

After she left, Chico and I moved into her home. It was the same house I had grown up in, so I knew the neighborhood. But by then, it had literally turned into the hood. What was once a vibrant neighborhood with manicured lawns and patio sets in the backyards had become a community riddled with abandoned homes and broken-down cars.

A growing number of crack heads had begun walking the

streets day and night. Luckily, our immediate neighbors remained the same and continued taking care of their property. The only upside for me was that it was a bigger place. But to Chico, whose whole family had lived in Daniel Payne, one of the most notorious housing projects in Birmingham for generations, it must have seemed like a move up.

What sold me on the idea of moving back into the old neighborhood was something that my friend, Renita, who was a nurse and still lived in the community, said.

"Lawayne, these kids need role models, somebody they can see getting up, putting on decent clothes and going to work every day."

When she put it like that it made good sense. After all, "It's not where you live but how you live."

One Sunday after church Chico and I had been lounging around the apartment. Excited about the move, we decided to go to Home Depot to buy paint and other essentials to spruce up the house before we moved in. We had a great time on the way talking about everything we wanted to do to make the place fit our personalities. When we got there the parking lot was packed so we circled it a few times before we could find a place to park.

We were both in a good mood from the great music and conversation we had enjoyed along the way. As we were walking into the store, I just happened to look down at Chico's feet and noticed he had on house shoes. That caught me off guard. I was not accustomed to any of my friends wearing house shoes out in public, especially Chico, who always had an eye for fashion and was always on point whenever we went anywhere.

"Are those house shoes?" I asked.

He laughed and said, "Yeah" with that bright smile as only he could flash.

I then asked, "Why are you wearing house shoes to the store? Are you serious?"

By this time I was ticked off, and so was he.

Where I come from, wearing house shoes to a store or anywhere outside the house was considered inappropriate. But to Chico, who grew up in the projects, it was perfectly fine. I tried to ignore it, but I couldn't. I guess I was more concerned about what his house shoes said about me than what they said about him.

The pride that my family instilled in me wouldn't allow me to accept house shoes or wife beater tee shirts as appropriate wear in public places like Home Depot. I stopped in my tracks just as we were about to walk in the door and said, "Let's go."

We hurried back to the car and drove back to the apartment without saying a word.

Chico got in bed and covered his head, and I don't think we said a word to each other for nearly a week. I tried speaking to him, but he just shut down completely.

Noted author and life coach Iyanla Vanzant once said, "Sometimes we don't know what other people are carrying in their heart because we don't talk; we assume."

I knew in my heart that Chico was the wrong man for me. That's not to say he was necessarily a bad man, just not the right guy for me. But because of my loneliness and determination to fix what I perceived to be his problems, I ignored my own feelings.

I don't think we were ever truly honest to each other about what we were really carrying in our hearts. All I really wanted was a "live-in teddy." I'm not exactly sure what he wanted.

When we moved into the house, I was amazed at how quickly he had put everything into place. We moved in on a Saturday, and when I left for work Monday morning, there were still plenty of boxes with lots of pictures, kitchen utensils and other odds and ends waiting to be unpacked. I ended up working a little late, so when I got off it was already dark. As I turned onto our street I saw something that I hadn't seen in years.

Our house was glowing.

The custom cream-colored designer drapes were pulled open with a swag design exposing the beautifully decorated home inside. A brightly colored abstract painting of African dancers hanging above the fireplace popped against the soft green walls. The contemporary crystal chandelier that hung above the glass dining-room table glistened under the soft lights. And the African masks and other art sculptures accentuated the warm golden-colored oversized sofa, chaise lounge and accent chair. Chico had my favorite cocktail sitting on the glass and wrought iron coffee table. It was in one of those fancy-stemmed glasses garnished with fruit and an umbrella. Soft jazz was being piped from the stereo and the smell of pork roast, cabbage greens and sweet potato yams flowed from the kitchen. It smelled like coming home to Mom's cooking.

As we sat there enjoying our cocktails, our meal and each other everything was perfect. Even though I was afraid the neighborhood crack heads were getting a bird's-eye view, I didn't have the courage to tell Chico to close the curtains because in my heart of hearts I knew it would start an argument or he'd do one of his shutdown or disappearing acts. So as our evening came to a pleasant end I turned out the lights. And we spent the rest of the night enjoying each other's company in our bedroom.

But the more Chico and I got to know each other, the faster the halo faded. No longer was he just my little "live-in teddy," he had become the man of my life. However, he was also a troubled man, in need of not only a partner but a mentor and a counselor.

I found Chico to be a chronic liar. We had been together about a year, and he was still dropping me off at my job.

That meant he was putting hundreds of miles on my car every week, but I didn't complain. After all, he was a black man working (BMW). In fact, he told me he had been with the company he worked for at least a couple of years. He said he had great insurance and that he was being considered for a supervisor's position.

I was paying all the bills on time, but one day I missed paying my phone bill. During those days we didn't have the convenience of paying online or calling in a debit card payment over the phone.

So I went downtown to a payment center. The place was always busy with people buying money orders, having checks cashed or paying all types of bills, including phone and utility bills. I must have stood in line a good 20 minutes watching a circus of characters come and go. When I finally got to the window I paid my bill and stood there waiting for the clerk to key my information into the system. I casually looked down on the counter behind the glass, where I saw a huge stack of checks that had apparently just been cashed. On the very top was a check from a temporary work agency payable to Chico Presley. The organized chaos surrounding me quickly came to a standstill and everything went silent for a moment. This was *my* Chico Presley, the same man with the good job that was showing so much promise.

That explained why he was off work so many days, because if they didn't need him, they didn't call him. When I asked Chico about it he lied at first and said it must have been somebody else. But later that night he came clean and told me he had been working with the temporary agency for years. He said he'd been hoping it would turn into a permanent position. I felt sorry for him because he was way too smart to be working a job that didn't even offer health insurance.

At the time, I was a bank operations supervisor. I worked in the cash management area where we processed payments for large corporations. There weren't any openings in my area, but there were a few positions available in the mailroom. I suggested that Chico apply for one.

I told him exactly what to write on his application. I even told him what to wear, what to say and how to conduct himself in the interview. Luckily, he got the job.

Even when Chico started working at the bank we were still sharing my car. The job was actually less than a mile from the house. So on the days when I'd have to work late, he would take my car and come back to pick me up or he'd just walk home.

One particular night Chico and I had just turned the lights out and gone to bed. We were snuggled in each other's arms when the doorbell rang. It startled me because we didn't typically have people stopping by unannounced, especially at 11:45 at night. I tried to get Chico to go to the door with me, but he wouldn't.

When I got to the door I looked out of the peephole, but I didn't recognize the face so I asked, "Who is it?"

"Is Chico home?"

"Chico?"

"Yes, is Chico home?"

"May I ask who you are?"

"Tell him Corvis."

"Chico," I yelled, "somebody named Corvis is looking for you."

"Tell him I'm asleep."

"He says he's asleep, man."

"OK, tell him I came by."

When I asked Chico about Corvis, he told me it was someone he grew up with in the projects. He said Corvis's family had moved away a couple of years ago, and earlier that day they had run into each other.

I asked him, "Are y'all friends?"

"No, not really. He's just a guy from the neighborhood."

Now, I may be a fool, but I'm not a damn fool. But because I didn't want to tick him off, I got back in the bed and just let it go.

After that incident, his stuff started getting really raggedy, and we started sliding further downhill. Chico would start a fight when it was time to pay bills. He'd notoriously go home to his mama to live on her dime. Then after a couple of weeks had passed, he'd come home to me with a sad story and an apology. And every time, I'd let him back in and take more of the same mistreatment.

But some occasions were harder for me to ignore, like when he gave me Chlamydia, and then tried to blame it on me. But we were practicing safe sex, and I was only sleeping with him. Perhaps for the first time in my life I was faithful, honest, dedicated and committed to one somebody. I was determined not to cheat on Chico the way Chazz and I had cheated on each other.

I don't know why, but I was determined that I was going to do everything in my power to make this the best relationship it could be. But no matter how hard I tried, Chico continued to push me to the limit.

I remember our first fistfight. I say *first* because there were many.

It was a beautiful afternoon. We had gone to the civil rights district and toured Kelly Ingram Park, a popular gathering spot in Birmingham during the civil rights era. The park is filled with cast-iron vignettes of statutes depicting scenes from the turbulent '60s. One is of dogs attacking young children. Another is of firemen turning their hoses on a crowd of people.

One display is a jail cell that represents the thousands of men, women and children who were arrested for their courage to fight for freedom and equality. At the end of our tour we sat near the reflecting pool.

From there we could see the Birmingham Civil Rights Institute, the statue of Dr. Martin Luther King Jr. and the Sixteenth Street Baptist Church. That's the church that was bombed early one Sunday morning by members of the Ku Klux Klan. When the smoke cleared, four little girls were the unfortunate casualties.

The explosion was said to be heard around the globe because it sounded the alarm to just how bad race relations were in Birmingham and throughout the South.

But Chico didn't believe their deaths were any more significant than the scores of other men, women and children who had lost their lives during the movement, especially the racially motivated killings of two young black boys that same day, just a few miles away from the church.

That may be true. But I'm reminded that there really is truth in the saying "It's not always what you say but how you say it."

And what Chico said had certainly rubbed me the wrong way.

Suddenly, reality was hitting me smack in the face. Here I was with a boy who was nearly young enough to be my son and neither of us had more than a physical attraction in common. For the first time I realized Chico represented things that I loathed. He was highly opinionated, overly aggressive and extremely manipulative. In retrospect, he reminded me of the cartoon character Daffy Duck—bitchy, clueless and capable of lying straight in your face without batting an eye. To make it plain, Chico was the kind of guy who'd swear with the deepest conviction that his mess doesn't stink.

As these thoughts and feelings about what and who I was involved with began to surface, I grew frustrated. No, I was downright angry at him for all of his ignorance, arrogance and stupidity. But even worse, I was angry with myself for falling in love with him.

Chico was the type of guy that I was always told to stay away from. I was taught to find someone with a good heart, treated me kindly and wanted something out of life.

All I wanted was for Chico to be that person. But he couldn't because he was the wrong man for me, and I was the wrong man for him. At the same time I questioned myself. Who was I to judge him just because he was different from me?

Again, confusion set in.

Still as we sat in that park, emotions raged within my mind and body to the point that I wanted to lash out and knock some sense into his head. I stood up and said, "Let's go."

By then he too was angry and rage showed on his face. When we got to the car, I remember pulling out of the parking space and onto the street. That's when he said, "That's stupid as hell, making it all about those girls when so many other people were killed too."

Before I knew it I had stopped the car in the middle of the

street, put it in park and punched Chico dead in his mouth. He hit me back, and instantly we were embroiled in an all-out fistfight in the heart of Birmingham's Civil Rights District.

By the time we got home the anger had escalated way beyond our control.

Chico came in and started putting his things in plastic bags, telling me to take him home. I wanted him and all of his stuff out of my house. I began throwing everything of his, including his clothes, toiletries and a frozen slab of pork ribs, onto the floor. But I refused to take him home.

Like Erykah Badu, I said, "I think you better call Tyrone."

That angered him to the point that he started punching holes in the walls and destroying artwork and a number of other odds and ends. Any sane person would have walked away from what had become an obviously volatile situation.

But he stayed, and I let him.

I guess I hadn't gotten sick enough of the fights, the lies, the cheating and the diseases. I just kept raising my tolerance level. He gave me Chlamydia twice, and it happened almost to the day a year apart. And yes! We were using condoms.

It was like he got it while celebrating an anniversary or something.

Even though in my heart of hearts I knew things between Chico and me would never get better, I didn't want to be alone. I didn't want to be in another failed relationship. I was determined to stay and make things work. I kept thinking that if I would do the right thing, he would do the right thing.

Unfortunately nothing was further from the truth. For months I had been hearing that Chico was a frequent visitor at the adult book stores around town. I didn't want to believe it because we were together all day at work. When we weren't together he was usually at choir rehearsal. But there were those times when he was upset and punished me by staying away for weeks at a time without even a phone call.

One day I just happened to be off of work taking a personal day. While I was home my phone rang. It was my friend Kym.

"Hey, what you doing?"

"Nothing."

"Well, I need you to do me a favor."

"Sure, what's up?"

"Hate to put you out, but I really need you to keep Jay for me while I go to the doctor."

"No problem, bring him on."

"Lawayne, are you sure it's not a problem?"

With a chuckle I said, "Girl, please, just bring him on. I'd love to see my nephew."

"OK, then we'll see you in a minute."

After Kym finished her appointment, Jay and I were going to meet her at our favorite Chinese restaurant for lunch. Kym had only been gone for about an hour when the phone rang.

"Hello."

"Hey, I'm ready."

"Oh, OK, we're on our way."

"Hurry up, Lawayne, because I am starving."

I laughed and said, "OK."

I quickly buttoned Jay up in his orange puff jacket, put his gloves and cap on and placed him in the car seat Kym had dropped off earlier. Then we headed off to the Chinatown restaurant.

I lived in the eastern area of the city, but where we were meeting was on the South side. Normally, I would take the interstate but because of traffic, I decided to take Tenth Avenue. That would take us right into the downtown area near where we were meeting up.

As I approached Eighth Avenue I could see the downtown adult book store. A black Camry in the parking lot looked a lot like Chico's. But there was no way that could be Chico's because he was at work. I passed on by the bookstore, but I still wasn't convinced that the car I had just seen parked on the lot was not Chico's. I ended up driving about a block past the store, but something kept telling me to turn around and go back. When I pulled into the lot I could see the black umbrella that he always kept in his back window.

I got a frog in my throat.

But what was I going to do with a baby in the car?

I couldn't take Jay into the adult bookstore. I could have sat there in the car and waited to see who came out and got in that car. Or I could park my car, lock the doors and ask God to watch over Jay just long enough for me to run inside to see if I saw Chico. I hate to say it, but I opted to leave Jay in the car. When I walked into the building I was on the main showroom. The fluorescent overhead lighting made the room look much brighter than I thought it would. About a dozen people were standing around perusing rows and rows of magazines, videos and other sex paraphernalia. I quickly scanned the room, but there was no sign of Chico. Just as I was walking into the hall where the private screening booths were, one of the doors opened . . . and Chico walked out.

We stared at each other, and he hung his head in shame as if to say, "Damn, I'm busted."

Neither of us said a word.

I quickly walked back out to check on Jay. He was safe and calm, but when Chico walked up to the car Jay started crying almost uncontrollably.

The only thing I said to Chico was, "I'll see you later."

When Chico walked away from the car I drove away. Almost instantly Jay stopped crying.

We went on to meet Kym at Chinatown. No doubt we had fried rice and hot-and-sour soup. But when I told her about what had just happened with Chico, I thought she was going to choke.

"Lawayne Orlando Childrey, I know good and damn well you ain't left my baby in no damn car."

After a good cursing out I asked for her forgiveness.

"Yeah, yeah, yeah, don't let that shit happen again."

After accepting my apology she wanted to know all the dirt that led up to the situation. At the end of the meal I cracked open my fortune cookie, and ironically, it read, "The most important thing in communication is to hear what isn't being said."

I thought, *Dang! How ironic.*

When we got home that evening Chico and I talked about what had happened earlier in the day. He said he had always had a curiosity about the bookstore but never had the courage to go in. So on his lunch break he said he decided to just give it a shot.

I knew he was lying, but I also knew he was young and was going to try any and everything out there.

Even though I've never gotten into the bookstore scene, it didn't mean he couldn't.

Besides, Chico was young and was bound to want to experience new things. He said that one visit was enough to curb his curiosity, and I ignored the truth.

The rest of the week was pretty smooth with Chico. He didn't get that arrogant attitude that he usually got when he was caught up in a lie. In fact, we were really cool all week. He even fixed a couple of romantic dinners. I remember thinking that maybe he's finally growing up and learning to appreciate what he has at home.

Friday night Chico and I were lying in bed watching TV. We hadn't been having sex because I really wasn't feeling him like that after catching him hanging in the bookstore, a known cruise spot.

Shortly after getting in bed he kept telling me, "I'm hot!"

I told him to turn the heat down.

He did, but he said he was still hot. He kept saying, "I'm hot, Wayne, I'm hot."

Suddenly, he jumped up out of the bed, got dressed and said he was going to the store.

I lay there for a minute, then it kicked in. Hot actually meant horny.

So I got up out of bed and threw on some jeans, a T-shirt and tennis shoes. As I was backing out of the driveway a thousand questions were racing through my head. *Where is he really headed? Was it all planned out? Who else is involved in what I now saw as some kind of conspiracy?*

My gut instinct was not to drive by the convenience store that was just a couple of blocks from the house. Neither was it to drive by his mother's house where he would often disappear to, especially when it was time to pay bills. I never even considered driving by his friend's house where he was known to chill for days when things went bad with us.

Instead, I drove by the adult bookstore where I had seen Chico in the beginning of the week.

It was about eleven o'clock that night, and there were only about five cars in the parking lot. One of them was Chico's.

As I parked the car, my heart was racing, the adrenaline was flowing and I knew there would be trouble. How could he do this to me again in the same week? In my mind, we had

155

never had any problems pleasuring each other sexually. Then I thought, could this be my fault? What could I have done to force him out of the comfort of my bed into the arms of a stranger from an adult bookstore?

As I was walking into the store to confront him he was walking out. A tall, slender, dark-skinned guy that I remembered from the clubs back in the day was walking out with him. Chico told the guy to go ahead and he'd catch up with him later. The guy got into his car and pulled off. Chico went back into the bookstore as if trying to buy time to get his story together.

I asked him, "What's going on?"

"What do you mean what's going on?" he said. "It's a free country. I can come here if I want to."

For the first time in my life I believe I understood what people mean when they say, "It cut like a knife."

Chico and I got into an argument right in front of the cash register. The clerk behind the counter told us that we needed to cut it out and that he was going to call the police. When we stepped outside I got up in Chico's face trying to question him and cursing him out at the same time.

As he pushed me off of him, I lost my balance and fell to the ground. In the process, I scraped my arms up really badly. They were dripping blood and began to swell. I cried out to the clerk for help. Chico and I continued to exchange words, but when the manager told us that the police were on the way, Chico jumped into his car and sped away.

In a flutter of flashing blue lights the police quickly arrived. I showed them the bruises I'd gotten from the fall. I also went over the details that led up to the fight and what happened in the heat of it all. They advised me to seek medical attention and suggested I could swear out a warrant for Chico's arrest through the magistrate's office.

I left Medical Center East about five o'clock that morning, totally fed up with Chico. I was sick and tired of all of the fussing, fighting, lies and emotional distress. I was tired of being taken advantage of and him running in and out of my life as he saw fit. The man I once viewed as an angel wrapped in the glow of love had now become a manipulative monster.

But to his defense, Chico only did what I allowed him to do. He didn't strip me of my dignity; I willingly gave up my dignity. But the mere thought of him upset me so much that it made me feel anxious and uneasy.

Filing the warrant with the magistrate's office was a slow, tedious process. I had to wait hours before anybody was even in the office to file the paperwork. When they finally got there I had to recount what happened.

After it was all completed the officer told me they would be making the arrest.

Days passed and the Birmingham Police Department still hadn't picked Chico up for the assault charge. I didn't know they wouldn't just go to his house and arrest him. But TJ told me the police would have to know exactly where he was before they would even attempt an arrest.

Chico had been dissing me and serving up so many attitudes at work that it was starting to become unbearable. So I called the police and I told them he'd be at work at 3 p.m. that day.

My heart was bleeding. I felt so misused and abused by this guy who had cheated on me from day one and had taken advantage of me in every way possible. I'm talking about the same man who put hundreds of miles on my car every week to get to his temporary job, and then told me he didn't have room for me in his car when he finally got his own.

Yes!

I wanted to see him humiliated just as he had humiliated me for nearly 3 years.

So around three o'clock I drove up to his job and parked in a spot where I could see the police escort him out of the building in handcuffs. The officers opened the rear door, placed him in the backseat and drove away.

I went to his mother's house and told her what had happened. All of his family said they understood why I did what I did.

They loved Chico, but they also knew just how big of a fool he was. Chico was released from jail sometime that night. Even though we continued seeing each other, the relationship was finally beginning to wear me down and I was looking for a way out.

THIRTEEN

WHEN IT HURTS SO BAD

TJ AND I have been friends since high school. He was all the things I considered myself to be—intelligent, sensual and passionate. Even though he didn't mind telling you whatever was on his mind, good or bad, he was still extremely popular and loved by many. TJ was a born leader, and I was always following him somewhere I had no business going, even in high school.

One of those forbidden places was an 18 and up club where the security guy didn't start checking IDs till ten o'clock. We'd sneak in early so we could party before curfew.

The Lighthouse was always hopping on Wednesday nights, and TJ was not about to miss out on the action.

It was the hottest club in town. People from everywhere made their way there just to get their groove on. I always imagined the Lighthouse to be Birmingham's version of New York's famed Studio 54.

Laser lights, sparkling mirror balls and feather boa-wearing drag queens were the stars of the show. Red, blue, green and yellow lights glowed on the dance floor to the beat of the music. Disco was hot, and the Lighthouse sizzled.

TJ graduated a year before I did and enlisted in the army. By the time we reconnected several years later, he had completed several tours of duty, including the hellhole of Iraq during Desert Storm.

While TJ was serving our country and experiencing unimaginable stress and valor, I was enduring abusive relationships and working unfulfilling jobs in retail and banking. So like me he had endured experiences that left him broken physically, mentally and emotionally.

When we started hanging out again it was like we never skipped a beat. We did everything together. I was right there for him and his family when his brother Randy succumbed to complications from AIDS. He was there for me when Cheryl died. And when Chazz died he held me up through the entire process, down to selecting the clothes I'd wear to the funeral. When I wanted to sit idle and wallow in my sorrow, he was quick to remind me to get up, get out and keep being strong.

TJ was the one who helped me pack up the apartment, load the truck and move all of my personal FX (belongings) that I didn't decide to give away after Chazz died. I could depend on him for almost anything. Including just lending an ear when I needed to vent or let off steam. During those days, TJ was an administrative assistant at a veterans' hospital. I was a bank supervisor.

Mondays were our off days. It had become a tradition for us to get together on those days for our weekly luncheon/bitch session/drinking/movie day. Normally, he would fry pan trout and make sandwiches. We'd eat salads, sip straw-berry daiquiris, piña coladas or some fabulous concoction that he'd mix when his creative juices were flowing.

TJ was an extremely generous guy, always helping any-way he could. If someone needed a place to stay or food to eat they could count on TJ. Entertaining people and show-ing them a good time was his specialty, and he always had lots of people coming and going from his apartment.

After a few months it became harder and harder to pin TJ down, which was shocking since he was basically a homebody. He started hanging with a new set of friends, and there was a noticeable change in his personality. It got to the point where he was always in a hurry and extremely evasive. So I asked him, "Where you been, man?"

"Just hanging with some friends."

"Who, TJ?"

"Lawayne, nobody you know."

"I know I don't know, that's why I'm asking."

"Just with some friends, Lawayne."

The weirdest thing is that he claimed he really couldn't stand these brand-new friends. He became more moody, developed a respiratory problem and was easily agitated.

After weeks of disappearing with his new crew he contin-ued to keep them a secret. TJ and I were still hanging out, but not like we used to. We were just like brothers who did everything together. So when he started hanging with peo-ple that he never had anything good to say about, I became more than a little concerned.

Every year for my birthday TJ would always throw me a lavish party, with lots of food, drinks and a handful of our closest friends. This particular year he decided not to. A couple of his new friends were also born the day before

Halloween. So instead of throwing me a party, he asked me to attend their party with him.

Around that time of year there is always a lot going on in Birmingham, like the Magic City Classic, a big in-state football rivalry between Alabama State and Alabama A&M universities. The whole week is filled with fun parties, parades, pep rallies, concerts and more. The morning of my birthday, I woke up early, got a fresh haircut, went to the mall and bought a pair of jeans and Timberland boots. I washed and waxed my ride until I could clearly see my reflection in it. I wanted to make sure I was ready for an evening of fun.

About eight o'clock, I picked up TJ. Our plan was to stop by his friends' party, leave there and go to the club to celebrate the rest of my birthday. If we didn't go to the club, we were gonna cruise the city checking out the tailgaters at Legion Field.

If Black America ever wanted to see Birmingham at its best, Magic City Classic weekend was the time to do it. Everybody threw a party so there would be plenty of options to choose from.

When TJ and I arrived at his friends' apartment complex, we sat in the car and talked for a minute so he could lay down the ground rules.

"Now, Lawayne, don't be in here acting like no li'l bitch. These are some grown-ass people, but they have been really nice to me. I'm just telling you this because I know how you can be."

He always thought I could act uppity at times so all I said was "OK." Then we walked up to the door.

After about two knocks a pretty young woman opened the door. Greeting us with a laugh and a hug she said to TJ, "I knew yo' ass was gonna be late. Git on in here."

He said, "Angela, Lawayne, Lawayne, Angela."

Angela said, "Oh, Lawayne, TJ talks about you all the time. Y'all are best friends, right?"

I said, "Yeah, we've been friends forever."

TJ chimed in, "Lawayne has been my very best friend since tenth grade."

Angela immediately started introducing me to the others in the room.

Her husband, Tony, was a tall, slender, light-skinned guy, neatly dressed with a fresh haircut. He was the pretty-boy type, like he could have pledged Kappa or Alpha when he was in college. Angela then introduced their friends Anthony, Mark and Curtis.

They all gave a nod or said something like "Hey, man, wuts up?"

I said, "It's all good."

As my eyes scanned the room and faces, I couldn't help but focus in on the coffee table.

What I saw nearly caused me to blow my cool. I was shocked to see what TJ had gotten into.

There were huge quantities of weed and crack cocaine scattered between the beer cans, ashtrays and cigarette lighters on the glass-topped table.

My first instinct was to turn the table over, grab my buddy by his neck and pull his butt out of that drug-infested hellhole. But I didn't.

Why not?

Because I'm Lawayne, and I thought I could handle any situation. So I sat there, trying to be cool as a cucumber on the outside. But on the inside I was as nervous as a kindergartner being dropped off at school for the very first time.

As we all sat around the living-room table, Tony was rolling a marijuana joint and lacing it with crack cocaine.

163

The first thing out of TJ's mouth was, "Don't give Lawayne any of that shit. He'll smoke his weed but don't give him any of that shit. He doesn't do that shit. And he ain't fixin' to start either."

My mind went back to when I had unknowingly smoked a joint laced with crack at my buddy Clint's house years ago. When I found out it was laced, it made me so mad that I stopped hanging with him. But it didn't seem to hurt me then, and I was now mad at TJ for saying what's best for me.

So I said, "I'll primo."

TJ said, "Lawayne, don't do that."

Not wanting to be outdone I said, "I'm good."

Looking back, it's easy to see how emotions play a huge role in our decision making. The logical me saw the risks and knew that the smart move was to leave. But the emotional me jumped right in with both feet. I saw it as a way to take my mind off of Chico, Chazz and all the other depressing things that were happening around me.

So there I was, smoking a crack-filled joint but unlike before, this time I knew what I was doing.

And I liked it.

I loved the way it made my lips tingle and the sexual rush it gave me. I was having such a good time smoking and drinking that I decided to head to the club at twelve instead of ten.

When twelve finally rolled around we were still drinking and smoking.

Tony and I were smoking crack laced in marijuana joints. TJ and a few others were smoking it off of a beer can that they had semi flattened, poked holes in, piled cigarette ashes over the holes and laid pieces of crack cocaine on top. While lighting the crack rock with a cigarette lighter they sucked the fumes through the part of the can you sip out of. Others were smoking theirs through a glass pipe filtered with steel wool.

About 1 a.m. we had smoked out, so we pooled our money together and bought another hundred-dollar chunk of the white devil. Needless to say, I never made it to any of the classic festivities. Instead, I spent my birthday getting stoned with my buddy and his friends that he claimed he could not stand.

After we finally smoked it all up, TJ and I headed back to our apartments. I dropped him off and went on up a couple of blocks to my South-side pad. After getting home I was so wired I couldn't sleep. I was nervous and jittery. All I could think about was the tingling on my lips from the cocaine.

After crashing sometime later that morning, I must have slept at least 8 hours straight.

They don't call it the white devil for nothing.

In a matter of days I found myself in a vicious cycle, hanging with all types of crack addicts. It was a lonely time for me.

Even though I had a decent job at the bank, I never felt I was living up to my full potential and things seemed to be getting bleaker by the day.

Many of my friends and loved ones had died from AIDS. I've tried to take a count of all the people I've known to die from AIDS. However, after I reached 100 I stopped counting. I had only been diagnosed with HIV, the virus that causes AIDS. But I felt it was only a matter of time until I'd be dead too.

Plus I was in another relationship which was perhaps even more physically and emotionally abusive than the first.

In addition, Mom had suffered another stroke which left her needing oxygen and a quad cane. She was depending on me more and more to help her do many of the things we often take for granted, like putting on clothes or combing our hair.

165

There wasn't anything I would not do for my mother, but I wanted to do more. I wished I made enough money to hire a full-time staff to take care of her the way she deserved to be cared for.

I had reached a point in my life where I felt I was a failure. Life's walls seemed to be closing in. I wanted to die.

But I was too much of a coward to run my car off of a cliff or point a gun to my head and pull the trigger. I actually hoped that I'd smoke so much cocaine that I'd burst my heart open.

So I upped my game. Instead of smoking laced joints, I started smoking crack off of a can. When that didn't work, I began smoking it out of a glass pipe. That way, I was ingesting what I'd hoped would be a lethal amount.

After several months of smoking crack, I found myself in situations that I never dreamed I'd ever be in. It was nothing for me to leave work and head straight to the crack house. It wasn't just the allure of the drug. It was also the stimulating conversations that took place there. That's where loneliness and depression can lead you.

The genius of some of those people blew me away. We talked about everything, from politics and religion to health care and economics. They came from all walks of life. Some were businessmen, while others were street thugs. Some were even housewives with children. There were no judges, only lost souls. Ironically, most of them didn't seem to think I fit in. I'd always get asked, "Why are you here?" They'd say, "Shouldn't you be somewhere doing something like teaching school or just doing something more productive with your life?"

But their words fell on deaf ears. In fact, I kept getting more deeply involved.

Night after night I was somewhere getting high by any means necessary. Even if it meant driving across town when

I was already high, taking a chance on getting arrested and going to jail.

My life had become nothing less than bizarre.

One night I'd been hanging out with a guy that I had met several weeks prior. Raymond was a truck driver with a beautiful wife and kids, but whenever we'd get high he'd want to freak. Not with his wife but a prostitute.

We checked into a seedy motel on the other side of town that was known for prostitution and drug deals. It was my first time ever checking into a place like that. Even in my insanity, I felt dirty. I was worried about who had been there and what they had left on the sheets and on the floor and chairs.

Raymond and I had been chilling in our room smoking half the night. We kept looking for a freak but never could find one. It was getting late, and I was starting to get tired and sleepy.

He finally found a young white woman, brought her to our room and was ready to get busy with her. I was just there for the high, but I was also somewhat of a voyeur. However, we had smoked everything up, and she wanted a hit before she would do anything.

Raymond had bought the first round. I was going to buy the second one. But I was so high that I could not physically move.

In a state of extreme intoxication, insanity and confusion I gave Raymond my debit card. I also gave him my pin number and told him to go get the money out of my bank account to buy an 8-ball. When he left, I realized what I had done and paranoia swept in. Not only had I given this man that I barely knew my debit card, he also had my car and access to my house. Like I had done so many times, in so many rooms before while I was getting high, I began to pray inside.

"Lord, save me! Lord, deliver me! Lord, take this away from me!"

Even through the deepest trials and struggles of my life I always kept the faith that God would come to my rescue, if I asked for his help.

After what seemed like at least an hour, Raymond made it back to the room. He gave me my debit card, receipt and keys, then quickly sat at the table to break up the crack rock. We hit the pipe a few times, and then he went and found the woman again. As soon as she got to the room my anxiety kicked in again. I started wondering if they were planning to rob me, or worse, hurt or even kill me.

After we took a few more hits, Raymond took control and told the girl to take her clothes off. He took his off too. I sat there still smoking and positioning myself in a way that I could watch what was about to go down. But when I saw him enter her without using a condom it sickened my stomach. I turned my head in shame.

I kept asking myself if this was what I'd been reduced to.

And again I began to pray. "Lord, save me! Lord, deliver me! Lord, take this away from me!"

That was the last night I saw Raymond. I often thought about him, wondered how he was doing, how he and his wife were doing, and if he had contracted anything that he had taken home to her.

That morning I felt so out of control. It was as if I had lost my way.

I needed a lifeline so I continued to pray and call upon the name of the Lord. I had to face my newest demons, so again, I reached out for the support of my family. I told my mother what was happening to me and how I had become addicted to crack cocaine.

She was shocked. And I was ashamed. I hated to burden her with this news, at a time when she was recovering from a series of strokes that forced her into disability retirement. I had recently moved her from Nashville back to Birmingham to take care of her.

With the help of intense therapy she had reached a point where she was able to walk taller. Her speech had also improved, and she was doing some of her own shopping. But she needed me there to help manage her business affairs and make sure she was taking her medicines on time every day.

Thankfully, through all of my insanity I was able to do that.

I was also able to maintain a certain degree of dignity, or at least pretend to anyway. Even my closest friends, business associates, neighbors and other family members didn't know the hell I was going through.

Somehow, I was able to keep my crack friends on one side of the fence and my real friends on the other. I never mixed the two.

Of course, Mom was more than a little upset when I told her about the horrific mess I had made of my life. But my mom has always been able to remain calm in times of distress. She wanted to know all of the who, what, when, where and whys of how I became addicted.

Mom believed I'd pull through, and that gave me strength. I've always known if I couldn't depend on anyone else when I needed them, I could always depend on my mother.

I had been there in her times of need. And again, she was there for me. Mom and I agreed that I needed to get counseling. As a matter of fact, she even helped me make phone calls to different addiction counselors in the area that would accept my insurance.

I called Delois who was herself an addiction counselor and a bit of a comedian.

"Bruh Chiiry, is you all right?"

"Yeah, I'm all right."

"Wayne, what's wrong? You don't sound like yourself."

"I'm not."

"Are you OK?"

"Lois, I'm strung out on crack."

"WHAT? Wayne, are you serious? Don't be playing with me, boy."

"Lois, I'm not playing."

"How long have you been using?"

"About 3 months."

"Wayne, we've gotta get you some help."

"That's why I am calling you. What should I do?"

She suggested that I go through my company's employee assistance program (EAP). She said it would be confidential and offer me some type of treatment plan.

I tried the EAP.

But after about three sessions with a counselor I was back out using. I guess I wasn't ready to tackle my demons. It was easier to hide behind drugs.

I've learned that when it comes to addiction everyone has their own bottom. Sometimes it comes in the form of being locked up in a jail cell. For others, it's the loss of a family member or good health. Still for some, the bottom doesn't come until you're 6 feet under.

Although I thought that last night with Ray was my bottom, it was not. The worst was yet to come.

One Saturday, Michael and I had been hanging all night. Michael was just the opposite of Angie and Tony. Even though he worked for a cleaning service, his clothes were always dirty, just like his apartment. His whole scene was weird and wild. I had even watched a man sitting on his sofa playing Russian roulette. He put the gun to his head, pulled the trigger and miraculously survived.

Michael seldom had money to pay his rent, utilities or his fair share in the dope game. To compensate, he would let people come to his apartment to smoke as long as they let him smoke with them. That's why I was usually one of the ones getting him high.

But by some strange circumstance he had come into some money and was getting me high this particular night.

Michael and I had smoked down to our last hit. So we set out on a quest to find more crack, but all of our usual contacts were sold out. We took to the streets in areas where people were known to sell it.

One of the places we ended up was Central City Projects. Central City was notorious for gangs, shootings, drug deals and drug busts. Michael thought he knew someone in the area who could hook us up.

So about two o'clock in the morning we drove into the parking lot. As Michael was getting out of the car to go knock on his buddy's door, two guys came up and asked a simple question.

"What are y'all looking for?"

Michael said, "We're looking for Skip."

One of them said, "Skip ain't here, man. What you need?"

Michael told the guy, "We want to get an 8-ball."

He said, "I can do that, but you'll have to come to my place."

After a brief glance and hesitation Michael and I decided to take the chance. However, there was one scary condition. The dealers wanted me to get out of the car and stand behind the garbage Dumpster until they got back. They said they didn't want the police to pull up and see someone sitting in a car.

One of them said, "It looks too much like a drug deal in progress."

So I got out of my car with the keys in the ignition and stood behind the Dumpster waiting for Michael to come back with the dope.

I waited so long that condensation formed on the car windows. I was terrified and thought long and hard about driving off and leaving Michael. I was also wondering if we were about to become the next victims to be found dead in Central City.

Finally Michael showed up with the dope. We quickly hopped into the car and he said, "Let's get the fuck up outta here."

I was still scared we'd get robbed, shot at or stopped by the cops. I didn't relax until we were completely out of the area. That's when he gave me a good look at the goods.

I said, "Dude, I know you've already broken off of this."

He said, "Man, you done lost yo' damn mind. Ain't nobody broke off shit."

But I knew he had because it was the smallest 8-ball I've ever seen.

Day was breaking.

I was tired and ticked off at the crap we had just gone through. All I wanted to do was go back to his place, get a good hit and go home.

Instead, Michael still wanted to find a freak to play around with. We rode around downtown, but everybody had already called it quits for the night.

So we drove out to East Lake, another notorious spot for hookers and whores. When we pulled into the motel parking lot there was a woman standing in the breezeway, but her back was facing us.

Michael rolled down the window and called out.

"Hey, Sexy."

Slowly she turned around, but she didn't look like a woman at all. Rather, more like a monster. She appeared to be someone in her mid fifties who had been rode hard. With dozens of nickel-sized bumps on her face and a mouth full of gapped teeth she looked like she had taken one too many sips from the witches' brew.

Just looking at her made me want to throw up. Michael seemed game to pick her up, but there was no way in hell that woman was getting in my car. Thank God I had enough sense to take control of the moment.

I knew then that it was time to take Michael to his apartment and get back to my own house.

When I got home I told Mom that I was back on drugs and that I felt so out of control. I had finally hit rock bottom and wasn't sure I could make it out. I called Delois and told her what had happened.

This time, we all agreed that I needed to be in an inpatient setting. That way, I could get the best treatment possible.

My employee assistance provider suggested I go to Medical Center East.

In the meantime, I called TJ and told him what I decided to do. Experience had taught him that the only way they would accept me that day was if I told them I wanted to hurt myself or someone else.

But the truth of the matter is that I *did* want to hurt myself. That's why I was doing crack in the first place. I'd hoped to smoke enough that it would burst my heart and I'd die.

After getting the approval from EAP, I knew I was going to

check myself into the hospital that day. But I also knew I had some things that I needed to get settled before I checked in.

One thing was to simply do laundry and clean up my bedroom. knew I didn't want to come home from the hospital to a messy house. And for the past few weeks I had let things pile up.

Also, I needed to pack a bag because I wasn't planning on leaving rehab until I knew I could enjoy life again without drugs.

Lastly, I had to take Michael's VCR back to him. He had given it to me to keep so he wouldn't sell it for crack. I don't know why, but many of the crack addicts I hung with all trusted me to take care of their personal belongings. They all knew that I wouldn't sell or give away any of their things for a high.

As I was doing laundry, Mom decided she would go pick up a few items from the store. Even though she was walking with a cane, she continued to make tremendous progress through therapy.

When she left, I sat in the living room. Watching TV and thinking about my situation, I began to pray.

"God, please deliver me from this dreadful addiction that has left me drained mentally, physically, financially and emotionally."

My prayers were perpetual.

As I sat on the sofa, a silver BMW pulled up. It was my buddy Chester. He and I had been friends for about 10 years. Chester was a light-skinned, clean-shaven brother with high expectations. He worked as an IT specialist for a major soft drink manufacturer. Chester was about 10 years younger than me and always called me his big brother. On any given day we could talk on the phone for hours about anything. We'd often get together for dinner or drinks or just hang out.

Unfortunately, we hadn't done any of those things in a while because of my drug addiction.

I had been avoiding Chester and so many of my other friends for nearly a year. I'd talk to them on the phone, but I rarely visited them or allowed them to come see me. I was ashamed of what I had become, and I wanted to keep that part of my life hidden from them.

Watching Chester walk up the sidewalk and onto the porch I began to have flashbacks. All I could think about were the lies I'd told him about why we couldn't get together for lunch or happy hour. I thought about all the times he invited me to go to church with him and I refused because I knew I'd be somewhere getting high.

By the time Chester rang the doorbell, all of the lies, all of the deception, all of the guilt and shame of what I'd become overtook me. Like a breached dam I broke down and cried hysterically. Opening the door, I became more emotional and began sobbing uncontrollably.

Chester held me in his arms and asked, "What's wrong Boo Boo? Why are you crying like this?"

But I couldn't say a word. All I could do was cry and cry and cry. My emotional breakdown must have lasted for at least 10 minutes.

As I was coming out of it, I felt a sense of relief. It felt as if I was being cleansed of not only the stench and filth of my crack addiction but also the lies and deceit that went along with it.

Even though my body was wet from the tears and my voice was quivering as I tried to talk, my friend held me close. As my body rocked back and forth and my hands and legs shook uncontrollably my friend still held me close.

When I eventually calmed down, I told Chester about all the hell my addiction had taken me through. Still he continued to hold me close and tell me everything would be OK. I apologized for abandoning our friendship, and he readily accepted.

When I began telling him my plan to check myself into a rehab that day, he insisted on taking me.

By that time, Mom walked back in from the store. She and Chester hugged, and he told her what had just happened. He said his good-byes but said he'd be back that evening about four o'clock to take me to the hospital, and he insisted that Mom ride with us.

Once Chester left I finished doing laundry and cleaning up my room. I packed a bag, cooked dinner and got dressed.

I was dreading having to go to Michael's house, but I knew I had to take him his VCR. Otherwise, it would be a while before he got it because I was sure I'd be in the hospital for several days.

When I got to his place, I gave him the VCR and told him I was tired of getting high and was checking myself into a drug rehab. To my surprise he laughed and said in a sarcastic tone, "You'll be back."

I asked, "Why would you say that?"

He said, "Don't worry about it. They all do."

I said, "Oh yeah? Well, I won't." I walked out the door, got into my car and never looked back again.

When we got to the hospital, Chester pulled up to the door to let Mom out of the car. He always treated her kindly. But since her strokes, all of my friends treated her with a special sensitivity. Mom and I went inside while Chester parked the car. We hadn't been in the waiting room 5 minutes before the receptionist called me to the window.

"What brings you to the emergency room tonight?" she asked.

I told her, "I've been smoking crack cocaine every day for

the past several weeks hoping to kill myself." And I told her, "I know if I don't get help it is going to happen."

They went ahead and placed me in a room. After what seemed like an eternity, a doctor finally made his way in, asking a series of questions.

"How long have you been using crack cocaine?"

"Why do you use it?"

"How much do you use?"

The questions went on and on.

After a few minutes, he was making plans for me to go to Hillcrest Rehabilitation Center. Hillcrest specialized in chemical dependency issues but was not necessarily considered to be one of the better hospitals in the area.

A young black nurse quietly whispered to me. "You have great insurance. Don't let them send you to Hillcrest; tell them you want to go to Baptist Montclair."

So I told them, "I'd rather go to Baptist Montclair."

When we arrived at BMC, they ushered me right in. And finally my reality quickly set in.

I wasn't expecting to be placed in a locked unit with people who had all types of emotional issues but I was. The doors were made of steel and the walls were an industrial shade of gray.

There was a security guard at the door who had to buzz people in and out. Many of the patients were in obvious distress. One man walked around telling everyone, "You are wearing the wrong color." Another was constantly beating the walls with her hands, and another carried on a conversation that escalated into an argument—with herself.

I was told by one of the nurses that when the doctor made his round the next day he would evaluate me and determine if I was ready to move to the detoxification unit.

After the nurse on duty checked everything that was in my bag for anything that could be considered contraband, they assigned me a room. As weird as it was, I knew I was in the right place. And I was confident that I wouldn't have to stay in that unit very long.

But I was still embarrassed for my mom and my best friend to see me locked up in what many would consider the crazy unit. After Chester and Mom got me all settled in, they assured me that I was in the best place possible and that I was going to be all right.

I put on a brave face for them, but deep inside, I was scared. I didn't know if any of those crazy people I had seen wandering the halls would find their way into my room trying to start anything. I was so nervous that I was given a sedative to calm me down and help me fall asleep. The next morning I woke up thankful that I had slept peacefully and without incident.

After breakfast and a few group activities like arts and crafts, the doctor finally came and evaluated me. That's when I was transferred to the addiction unit on the sixth floor.

Once there I was pleased to find there were no locks on the doors, and I was free to leave at any time. But the thought of leaving never crossed my mind. This was the first time in months that I felt safe from not only myself but also from the drug that had bound me. It was such a relief.

I had become a slave to crack, but now I was in a position to declare my freedom and take back what God had given me—my life.

I was determined to stay in the detoxification unit for at least a week in order to get clean and sober. Through a series of group meetings, I was forced to look at my addiction honestly and realistically. The goal was to help change my attitude about drug use. I knew I was sick, and I was never in denial about the seriousness of my problem. I wanted to get well and was determined to do just that. But in order for it to work, I had to be brutally honest with myself and everyone else in my life. Drugs were only part of my problems.

At the end of the first day, I wanted to call my supervisor, Monica, at work to let her know that I wouldn't be in for at least a week. I knew Mom had called and told her I was in the hospital and they were running tests to see exactly what was wrong with me. But in my heart of hearts I knew I needed to tell Monica the truth.

Nearly 2 decades have passed, but I can still remember the conversation like it was yesterday. As I dialed the number, my hands started shaking, my heart was racing and I started sweating profusely. After the third ring I heard her voice.

"Lockbox."

"Hey, Monica, it's Lawayne."

"Lawayne, hey, how are you doing?"

I could hear the excitement and concern in her voice.

"I'm OK, I guess, but I'm in the hospital."

"Yes, your mom called and told me you were having some issues with your stomach."

"Well, yeah, I am in the hospital, and I do have a nervous stomach, but it's deeper than that."

She said with what sounded like a mix of laughter and concern, "What are you talking about, Lawayne? You *are* going to live, aren't you?"

"Yes, I'm going to live," I said, "but I'm not just in a hospital."

"What do you mean?"

"I'm in a rehab."

"A rehab?"

"I'm in a drug rehab."

She laughed. "Lawayne, stop playing."

"I'm not playing."

"But your mom said—"

Before she could finish I said, "Yes, I know what my mom told you, but I had to call and tell you what is really going on."

She asked with a sense of disbelief and a stutter, "What-what-what are you talking about, Lawayne?"

I explained to her how over almost the past year I had been strung out on crack cocaine.

"Lawayne, stop playing."

"Monica, I'm not playing."

I sensed a cautious amount of disgust.

"Lawayne, I have family members on that stuff. They've been in and out of rehabs. You're not gonna be able to get off of that stuff."

I said, "Monica, I hear ya, but that's not the case with me. I'm gonna beat this."

She said, "OK, Lawayne, but you know I'll have to tell Joe about this."

Joe was her manager.

"Yes, I know."

"OK, call me back and keep me posted. Lawayne, Lawayne, Lawayne . . . I don't believe this. You take care of yourself."

"I will, Monica, I will."

When I called Monica back the next day, she told me that Joe said he was proud of me for having the courage to face my fears and seek treatment. The only thing he asked was that I not make it a public issue by discussing it with the other employees. But he assured me that I had his full support.

During my group therapy and individual counseling sessions I learned how to recognize the triggers that made me want to get high. For me, it was a laundry list of things, including my concerns with my mom's failing health.

She was a 10-year survivor of lung and brain cancer. It all started with her pack-a-day cigarette habit. Since then, she had a series of strokes that left her partially paralyzed and dependent on me to help manage her life.

I was happy to do it without any hesitation. In fact, I took great care of my mother, making sure she had everything she needed. But it always puzzled me when people would say, "You're such a good son."

It's all I knew. There was no way I could ever turn my back on her. But it was stressful not knowing if or when the next stroke would occur or how severe it would be.

The counseling sessions forced me to take a close look at every aspect of my life. That included the fire, the sexual abuse, growing up with an alcoholic stepfather, my promiscuity and failed relationships, including the one I was currently in with Chico.

Even though there were so many skeletons in my closet I think my failed relationship with Chico was the straw that broke the camel's back.

While we both had our share of problems with anger management, I had a major secret that I had not shared with him. I think it was because I was afraid he would react violently to the news. But if I was to get brutally honest and open with myself and the group I would have to bite the bullet and tell him. However, I had to make sure it was the right time.

When I called to tell Chico I was in a drug rehab, it was the first time I had spoken to him in over a week. I had tried reaching out to him several times, but like so many times before, he wasn't answering my phone calls. That's because he was doing one of his famous disappearing acts.

Although I knew I needed to share this secret with him, I also figured there were plenty of secrets he was keeping from me. When I told Chico I was in the hospital, I had not yet found the strength or the courage to tell him he was a big part of the reason I was there. I thought it would start a fight and from that point on, I was trying to figure out what would be the best time to address our issues.

Chico came to the hospital the very next day, which was the Fourth of July. He came strutting down the hall wearing red, white and blue floral-printed shorts, a blue tank top and a pair of sandals with the piece that slides between the big toe.

When I first saw him my heart started racing, my whole body, including my face and hands, started shaking, and it felt like a truckload of butterflies were in my stomach. As they fluttered their way up my chest, it felt like they had gotten trapped in my throat, making me feel as if I was choking. I felt like I was going to die.

I was finally able to settle down enough to have a conversation with Chico, but the hour-long visit seemed like a never-ending nightmare.

It wasn't his physical appearance that made me feel so uneasy being around him. Instead, I think it was finally obvious to me that Chico was never going to be the man I wanted him to be. At last, I realized that the two of us were totally different and that he would never fit into the life I envisioned for myself. As sick as I was, the core of who I was inside was still there.

During our visit he asked why I was in the rehab unit. I explained all about the drugs and how they were also treating me for emotional distress. But I didn't have the courage to tell him that our relationship was a big part of my problem. He was totally surprised that I had been using drugs for nearly a year and he didn't even know it.

Part of the reason he didn't know is because he disappeared so much that we didn't spend much quality time together. But when we were together I hid my addiction.

Chico could always be the sweetest guy. He even helped me care for my mom. That day he was bearing gifts of food that he and his mother had cooked for the holiday.

He brought BBQ ribs and chicken, potato salad, baked beans, corn on the cob and cold slaw. And as always, he laid it out with a grin on his face. Whenever Chico would flash that dazzling smile I'd melt. However, this time I didn't. In fact, this time it felt like my heart had frozen.

Even though he seemed concerned about my addiction and my emotional state of mind, I couldn't help but think of all of the times he cheated on me, left me stuck with all the bills and abandoned me for weeks at a time.

The mere thought of him began to make me nervous.

But Chico remained in rare form, hanging around, being attentive, even straightening up my room and putting the left-over food in the refrigerator down the hall in the kitchen.

When he got ready to leave he told me he was praying for my speedy recovery, and he'd be checking on me. He then walked up to me, slowly stuck his hand out and asked me to stand up. When I did, he wrapped his arms around me, held me tightly, licked my lips and kissed me with what seemed like every fiber of his being.

As he removed his arms from around my waist he slipped his hands in my hands, took a step back and whispered four simple words.

"I love you, Wayne."

Out of habit I whispered, "I love you too."

As I watched Chico walk down the hall to leave the unit, my knees buckled, my heart began to race and those butterflies filled my stomach again.

The next morning I explained to my psychologist, Dr. Dan, that every time I thought about Chico I'd get that seasick feeling. I'd always end up feeling like I was choking to death.

It was one of the most frightening things I'd ever experienced. I had never felt that way before, and it was getting worse. Dr. Dan diagnosed me as having an anxiety disorder. He explained that what I was actually experiencing was a panic attack.

It's almost impossible to explain what it feels like unless you've actually had one. And they started happening all the time. Even when I wasn't thinking about Chico I started having panic attacks.

I could just be watching TV, or in a group session, or doing an assignment from one of the classes, then all of a sudden a panic attack would come on. Dr. Dan started me on medication to help stabilize my mood, but he also taught me some therapeutic exercises to help me relax and face my fears.

One thing he instilled in me is that whatever I thought was going to hurt me couldn't hurt me because it wasn't a big old elephant—just a little bitty squirrel.

I kept telling myself that until I believed it.

"It's not an elephant, it's only a squirrel."

I still find myself having to say it even to this day: "It's not an elephant, it's only a squirrel."

Another tool he taught me was deep abdominal breathing. I'd close my eyes, take a deep breath through my nose and fill my belly up like a balloon. I'd hold it there for several seconds. Then, I'd calmly, slowly and very deliberately blow it out. I'd do about 10 repetitions.

It took a minute to get adjusted, but after a while I caught on, and they really started helping me calm down, and that feeling of anxiety and fear would ease away. What was supposed to be a week in the detox unit turned out to be more than 3 months of intense therapy. During that time, I was on a dual tract for drug addiction and emotional behavior.

In the mornings I'd participate in the drug addiction support program that used the 12-step approach. It helped me recognize the situations in which I was likely to use cocaine, how to avoid those triggers and how to cope more effectively with a whole range of problems and behaviors associated with drug abuse.

That program was filled with mostly straight men from all walks of life, and even though we were all different, we were bound together by our desire to live a clean and sober life.

It was therapeutic to hear their stories, which were so similar to mine. It also helped me to understand my addiction.

I'm not an alcohol addict or a pill addict or a food addict or even a cocaine addict. When it's all said and done . . . I'm just an addict. Thank God it's been more than 20 years since I used cocaine, but my recovery didn't start until I admitted I was powerless over my addiction and that my life had become unmanageable.

In addition to working the 12-step program, I was also receiving therapy for depression, anxiety, and psychological trauma that had plagued me since childhood. Unlike the addiction tract, the emotional tract at Baptist Montclair was filled with all types of women.

They included the 90-pound white women from Mountain Brook and the ghetto fabulous sistas straight from the hood.

As a matter of fact, I was the only man in the group. Nearly every afternoon we talked about everything imaginable, from posttraumatic stress disorder to codependency to bipolar disorder to the loss of loved ones.

The beautiful thing about group therapy is that there were no outsiders. We were all on the same team, and we capitalized on that camaraderie by opening up to each other.

In the book of James, chapter 5 verse 16, it says "Confess your faults one to another, and pray one for another, that ye may be healed."

So that's what we did.

We shared, we listened, we prayed and we even gave advice. Sometimes we came up with some terrible ideas, but we meant well. But whether the ideas were good or bad, talking to other people with the same problems was extremely beneficial. One of the tools that I learned to use in group therapy is called timeline therapy. The process is simple yet powerful. We'd take a piece of butcher paper, draw a horizontal line down the center and divide it up into 10-year intervals.

On the top of the line we'd place all of the past experiences that made us feel good in life or that impacted us in some positive way. On the bottom of the line we'd write all of the negative experiences or events that adversely affected us.

The life timeline is probably one of the most powerful tools I've ever used. It forced me to take a close look at all of the things that helped shape my life from the day I was born to where I am now.

It helped me to connect the dots of being born to a single mother, to witnessing a relative die in a house fire to being sexually abused by my stepfather.

The bottom of that timeline was crowded.

Of all the experiences I had written on that life timeline, more than three-quarters of them were negative.

Because I had never had therapy or talked to anybody

about any of it, I realized that I kept it bottled up inside far too long. All that junk had built up until I tried to release it by engaging in unhealthy addictions. But with the grace of God, that life timeline helped me get a good look at where I had been, and more important, where I was headed, if I did not start to turn things around.

Nothing was clearer to me. I had to deal with the issues, face my fears and begin to create a new life filled with new dreams and goals for myself.

In the process, I forgave all of those who had ever trespassed against me. In addition, I also forgave myself for all the wrong I had ever inflicted upon myself and others.

I once saw a movie called *The Josephine Baker Story*. There was a line in that movie that was so powerful to me that I've never forgotten it.

"We all wake up at different times, but we do wake up."

I believe that just as I believe the words of the Serenity Prayer which American theologian Reinhold Niebuhr composed decades ago, *"God grant me the serenity to accept the things I cannot change; courage to change the things I can; and wisdom to know the difference."*

Inpatient rehab gave me much more than my health. I was able to focus, without temptations or distractions. It gave me the courage to discover things about me that I never knew existed.

I realized that not only was I struggling with addiction, I was also entangled with the desire to gain power and control over my intimate partners.

The key to overcoming my problems was by talking about it with people who had been in abusive relationships similar to mine. Hearing their stories helped me to see the person I had become.

While I truly believe in psychological therapy and other support programs, such as Narcotics Anonymous, I honestly believe God delivered me from my crack cocaine addiction the day I checked myself into the hospital.

Allow me to rephrase . . . The day I realized I was powerless over my life and that I was destroying it in the process, God heard my prayer and in that moment, *he* delivered me from my addiction.

"Thank you, Lord, for your tender mercy."

Therapy gave me a new boldness.

The day I left rehab I went home and did something that most people take for granted. I bought some short pants and wore them. It was a major move for me because as big as I am, I've always had bird legs.

Oh yeah, I had big pretty thighs but little calves and tiny little ankles, so I would never wear shorts. After that, I think I wore shorts throughout the rest of the summer and into the winter.

That same night, I went to Chico's house to tell him the secret that I had kept from him since the day we met.

When I got to his house his mother greeted me at the door. She was glad to see me, and I was just as glad to see her.

I loved Gina, and although she was only a few years older than I, I looked up to her more as a mother figure rather than an equal. I talked to her about my time in the hospital and how it had helped me to deal with the mountain of emotional stress that I'd been under. She commended me for having the courage to get the help I needed and encouraged me to continue seeing my therapist.

After talking with her for a few moments I made my way back to Chico's room.

His door was closed as usual so I knocked. He knew I was there, but he still liked to play like he didn't have a clue.

After a couple of more taps he said, "Come in."

When I walked into his room he jumped up out of the bed, ran to me and gave me a big hug. That wonderful smile and kiss seemed to last a good 5 minutes.

He grabbed me by my hand and led me to sit on the bed with him. Gazing into my eyes, he said, "Baby, I'm so glad you're out of the hospital. I have missed you so much. Are you feeling better? You look great."

It was a magical moment that I did not want to end because deep within, even with all of his messed up ways, I loved Chico. But I knew if this love was to really grow I had to tell him a really big secret, and I had to do it that night, just as I had promised myself I would.

As we sat there in a deep embrace, I gently pulled away but continued to hold his hands, rubbing them softly and lovingly.

I stared deeply into his eyes until I could see my face and his soul. And then I asked, "Baby, do you love me?"

"Yes, Wayne, of course, I love you."

"Baby, I love you too, but there is something I really need to tell you."

The mood changed, we continued to hold hands, but I could see the expression on his face turn from joy to deep concern, and he said, "Baby, what's wrong?"

"Chico, there is something that I've wanted to tell you for a long time, but I never had the courage to do so until now."

I went on to say, "I hope you won't hate me. And I pray that you will understand and that we can continue to be lovers."

The tension swelled and as tears began streaming down

his face, he held my hands so tight that he was squeezing them.

I started sweating and feeling like I was going to have another anxiety attack, but I was determined to get it out.

I said, "Baby, I'm so sorry for just now telling you this, but I've been in denial for a very long time, but I'm not anymore."

He forcefully said, "What is it, Wayne?"

That's when I finally told him. "I know we've always used condoms. And you've always tested negative. But there is still something I need to tell you."

"Wayne, what is it?"

"I am HIV positive."

My heart stopped beating. The look on his face turned to stone.

"What?" he asked. "You're HIV positive? Wayne, how long have you known this?"

Tears continued streaming down his face. I tried to wipe them, but he only pushed my hands away.

By then I was holding him trying to comfort him. I pulled him closer to me. Both our faces and bodies were wet from the tears that were pouring like rain.

"How could you do this to me?" he said.

I continued apologizing, and suddenly he pulled away from me and screamed, "Get out! I never want to see you again. Get out!"

I quickly left. I thought we'd talk about it again after the news soaked in. But Chico and I didn't talk for about 3 weeks, and it was beginning to wear on me. I was miserable without him. I know God delivered me from the addiction of crack cocaine. But I still needed the help of my therapist to achieve my complete healing.

While I had made tremendous progress battling

codependency and abandonment issues, it took years of sitting on Dr. Dan's sofa, pouring out my soul, to attain the wholeness that I desperately needed.

I was fighting for my life, but I knew in order to continue making progress I had to keep the faith, even during my struggles.

Dealing with codependency and getting over Chico or any other bad relationship was probably the toughest challenge I'd faced up to that point. I needed intense weekly therapy sessions with Dr. Dan just to deal with the abandonment and rejection I received from Chico.

The breakup was so painful that I didn't think I would ever be able to go without calling Chico, even if it meant having him hang up in my face or not answer my calls at all. I had daydreams of him coming back to me.

Dr. Dan was so patient, and his advice was so useful. When I'd leave his office, I felt I could make it without Chico. But in between visits to Dr. Dan, those feelings of desperation would creep back in. And I'd have that feeling of abandonment all over again.

Just like I had been through detox for crack addiction, I needed a detoxification from Chico.

One of the people God sent my way to help guide and support me during those times when I couldn't see my psychologist was Gwendolyn Hagler.

Right from the start she was there, holding my hand and cheering me on, telling me I could make it.

Gwen and I had met in rehab and instantly hit it off. She was about the same age as Mom.

On the surface, we were the least likely candidates to develop an enduring relationship, but God had put us together. When I first laid eyes on her, I said to myself, "What is this beautiful, jazzy woman doing in here?"

She was about 5 foot 7, petite and casually dressed. But she had a certain quality and style that gay men appreciate in women.

I kept thinking there is no way she could be a crack addict. As it turns out, her drug of choice was the prescription pill Lortab.

Yes, rehab taught me that it doesn't matter what you're addicted to. Addiction does not discriminate. In the end, an addict is just an addict. You can be hooked on anything: booze, food, sex, cocaine, money, clothes, jewelry, work, even people. It's all the same if it's controlling you. After 4 months of therapy ended, Gwen and I remained close.

But I never ever saw her as an addict, only a friend and confidante.

In fact, our relationship grew deeper and deeper. She helped me to deal with Chico and continue the work we had begun in rehab. I trusted her unconditionally, and even though she was in therapy, it turns out that she was a licensed therapist herself.

Gwen is the person who helped me to open up to the possibility of therapy. One day in rehab we were sitting in the hall, and she asked me point-blank, "Are you gay?"

I knew then if I was really serious about my recovery I had to answer the question and I had to do it truthfully.

From that day on, we began learning more about each other, including my troubled relationship with Chico as well as my past history with Chazz and a long list of others.

When I told Gwen that I had finally told Chico about my HIV status and how he reacted, she wasn't surprised. But I know she was troubled that I was stressing over a man who obviously was the wrong man for me. So she started asking me, "What is it about him that you can't do without?"

Before I could answer she'd tell me, "Don't say anything now. Take a few days to just let it marinate."

That scenario of questions and answers went on and on, and even continues to this day. She had me do an exercise that was so powerful that I still use it when I need to make serious decisions in life. All it involves is taking a plain sheet of paper and drawing a line down the center.

On one side she had me to write all of the things I loved about my relationship with Chico. On the other side, I had to write all the things I hated about it. When I did the work I had used three sheets of paper. The things I hated took up all three sheets. The things I loved only had about six things on one sheet of paper. It didn't just happen overnight, but after about a year, I eventually began to let go of Chico.

FOURTEEN

WHERE DO WE GO FROM HERE?

AFTER CHICO AND I finally called it quits, I took about a year just learning to enjoy myself, by myself. But I'll never forget running back into Isaac.

It was a beautiful warm sunny day, and I had just dropped some letters off at the South-Side Post Office. My hair was freshly cut, my body was tight and I was feeling like I could do anything since I dropped that 185 pounds of baggage named Chico.

Isaac and I had met right after Chazz died, and I was trying to heal the pain with occasional nighttime company. When we got together then, I thought Isaac was a cool guy. He was about 5 foot 10, 165 pounds, with smooth chocolate skin and dreamy-brown eyes. I was already nervous bringing a stranger into my home. But when we started to get intimate, he took his shirt off and I saw bumps. They reminded me of the lesions that Chazz had on his back and chest before he died of AIDS.

I guess it's true what they say, "Time brings about a change, and time brings a change about."

With all the stuff I'd been through I'd finally learned not to judge a book by its cover. Despite my hesitation, Isaac had actually left a good impression on me. But at that time, I had just lost a lover to AIDS and wasn't mentally prepared to deal with any more illnesses. As I was coming out of the post office, Isaac was headed inside with a cute little curly-headed boy. I assumed the young preteen must have been his son. When my eyes met Isaac's, I could feel sparks happening between us. I wanted to go ahead and tell him how glad I was to see him again. Because he had stayed on my mind, I had even asked friends if they knew him or how I could find him. They all came back void. But that day in the post office parking lot I played it cool. We chitchatted for a while, and I asked him if he'd like to get together sometime.

He said, "Sure."

As he was writing out his number I told him, "You have a very handsome son."

Smiling and rubbing the young boy's head he said, "He's actually my cousin, but he may as well be my son because he's always with me." We laughed, and he promised to call me later.

Our first date was a movie that Sunday night. I have forgotten the name of it, but I can still remember what Isaac was wearing when he picked me up. It was a light gray cable knit turtleneck sweater, charcoal tweed slacks and a pair of black boots. I knew instantly that we were hitting it off because we had natural chemistry that made for easy conversation. We talked about our love for God and man and how we both wanted to leave the earth a little bit better than we found it. He was an X-ray tech with dreams of someday owning his own massage spa.

We discussed our love for the arts, whether it was theater or dance or charcoal etchings or clay sculptures. We talked about all the places we'd visited or wanted to see. It was a perfect night, and I was really feeling this man. After the movie, we went back to my place. Mom was staying with me because she was recovering from another mild stroke and couldn't stay by herself.

When we got home, I introduced them and they talked for a while until Mom retired to her bedroom.

In the meantime, Isaac and I sat in the living room watching TV and talking about everything from our mutual friends, to our families, to our jobs. By the end of the night I knew things could eventually get serious. After all, I was already turned on by his intellect, charm and sex appeal.

Drawing on all of the strength I'd gained from therapy, I decided not to beat around the bush. That's when I told Isaac, "I am HIV positive." If he was shocked he didn't show it. He remained cool, calm and collected. I'm sure he must have been disappointed. But all he said is that it didn't matter to him that I was positive. He still enjoyed my company and wanted to be with me as long as we played it safe. Just hearing those words felt like I had struck gold. Here was a man willing to love me, HIV and all.

About midnight, Isaac and I decided we needed to bring the date to an end. We both had to get up and go to work in the morning. As he was leaving we paused at the door and gave each other a big hug. I looked down into his dreamy-brown eyes, held his chin in my hand and gently kissed his lips good night.

As I closed the door, I couldn't help but think, "Finally, this is the one."

When he left I went back to Mom's room just to check on her. She was a known night owl, so it was common for her to be in bed watching TV all times of the night. I asked if she had taken her medicine or if she was hungry. She said she was good. That's when she asked, "What did you say his name is?"

I said, "Isaac, Isaac Ganson."

She said "Gaston as in AG Gaston?"

AG Gaston was a well-known entrepreneur in Birmingham. He created WENN radio, one of the first black-owned radio stations in the country. He also owned a bank, a business school, an insurance company and a motel. The AG Gaston Motel had housed just about every famous black person who visited Birmingham during the civil rights era, including Dr. Martin Luther King Jr.

I said, "No, ma'am, I didn't say Gaston, I said Ganson."

She said, "Well, I don't care what his name is. There's something about him that I really don't like."

That caught me off guard so I asked, "What did you say?"

"There is just something about him that I don't like." She said, "He seems too snooty or something."

I knew my mother was very protective of me. I remember the conversation she had with Chazz when they met. She told him straight out of the box, "You be good to my son. And remember, if you fuck over him, you will have to deal with me."

Mom was already feisty, but the strokes made her even more vocal about things that didn't sit well with her. But I think because she had watched me go through so much drama with Chazz and Chico, she was even more determined to shield me from unnecessary strife. Although I appreciated her concern, I could handle my own affairs.

I told her, "I know you love me. But, Mama, I'm a grown man. Although you may not like the people I decide to bring into my life, I insist that you at least respect them and not talk down to them."

From that day on she never said another negative thing against Isaac to me. In fact, she grew to love him dearly.

Over the next couple of months Isaac and I were doing almost everything together. I'd often pick him up from work and we'd have lunch in the park or at a cozy little restaurant near our jobs. Every Friday night was our full-fledged date night for a dinner and a movie.

The first time we made love was after one of those movie nights. We had both had a few drinks, our testosterone was raging, we were in love and we found each other irresistible. As we drove back to my place we couldn't keep our hands off of each other. When we got there, the house was dark. Isaac went downstairs to my bedroom, and I went upstairs to check on Mom. She was sound asleep. So I pulled the covers up over her shoulders and gave her a good night kiss on the forehead.

When I got to my room, Isaac was lying across the bed facedown in black bikini underwear watching TV. What a surprise!

Yes, we had been dating for a while. But we had decided to put sex off until we knew we were right for each other. And what we had was not mere lust but love. And love it was. What I felt for Isaac went way beyond anything I could have imagined real love to be. He was in my every thought, my every dream. I loved shopping with him and for him. I couldn't help but hold his hand or touch some part of his body when we were together. It was nothing for me to take a bite off his plate when we were having dinner in a restaurant. I could complete his sentences, and he could complete mine. Every day I prayed that God would continue to lead, guide and bless him abundantly and bless the love that we had found in each other. I felt miserable when we were apart, but all was grand when we were together. For the first time in my life, I saw a real opportunity to build a future with someone I loved.

So when I undressed before him and gently lay my body across his, it was in love. When I tenderly kissed the back of his neck and lightly nibbled his earlobe, it was all love. As I slowly ran my tongue down the small of his back, it was all in love. And in that moment, our hearts, bodies and souls became one. After what seemed like hours of passionate and safe lovemaking, we fell asleep in each other's arms.

I was the first to awaken, and I gently whispered in his ear, "I love you."

He opened his eyes, pulled me close, kissed my lips and quietly whispered, "I love you too."

But even when it comes to love, things are not always easy. Just as my mom didn't really care for Isaac at first, I don't think his mother particularly cared for me either. They lived together. One of the first times I met her she went slap off on me for playing with their dog named Max. He was a jet-black lab and chow mix, and even though he didn't take well to most people, he and I got along just fine. One day he was jumping up on me in a playful mood, and Isaac's mom told him to stop. I said, "Oh, he's all right, we're just playing."

"You don't tell me about my own dog," she retorted. "If I say stop, I mean stop."

It was an uncomfortable feeling for a moment, but I realized that she was probably just figuring out that her son and I were more than just friends and that I had been to her house without her knowing about it because her dog was so cozy with me. That was totally out of character for Max because he

199

didn't like too many people. With his ferocious bark and short temper he would scare the heck out of anybody that he didn't know.

Just as Mom began warming up to Isaac, his mom eventually began warming up to me. She'd even invite me over for holiday dinners and other family gatherings. It got to the point where I really enjoyed his entire family and his girlfriends, Whitney and Madison. Whitney was a schoolteacher in Miami. In fact, she started an in-home school for a very well-known sports legend there who had at least a dozen children. She was a great girl, with a great smile, hips for days and a personality that made anyone feel special.

Madison lived in Charlotte with her husband Blake, a big-time sales executive with a Fortune 500 company. I grew up in the same inner-city neighborhood as Blake, so it was good to see that a kid from the hood had gone on to build a great career for himself.

Whenever we were in Charlotte or Miami, we'd always visit, and when they'd come home to Birmingham, we'd always spend quality time together.

Isaac and I were having a great time mixing and mingling our lives with the lives of our families and friends. After about a year, I decided Mom was well enough to live on her own again. I mean she was driving, cooking, doing all of the things healthy people do. So I got an apartment on the South side of town. It was just 10 minutes away, so I could get to Mom quickly whenever she needed me.

When I decided to get the apartment, I talked it over with Isaac just to make sure he was on board. But then again, why wouldn't he be? We were already spending every day together, late into the night, and this would give us a real place of our own, a place where we could be totally relaxed and free to simply enjoy each other. He loved the idea, and he loved the neighborhood. The apartment was nestled along the hillsides of Red Mountain directly across from Rushton Park. It was the type of community with high-rise apartments next to antebellum homes and sidewalk cafés. It was a real mix of characters, too. It was common to see people walking their dogs at any time of day or night, and you didn't blink an eye if you saw a 60-year-old man rollerblading in a tutu.

Our apartment even had a bird's-eye view of the Highland Golf Club. It's the same course where Tiger Woods had taught a golf clinic to local school kids.

When moving day rolled around, all Isaac had to do was bring his clothes. I already had all of the furnishings, linens and cookware we'd ever need. When he got there empty-handed, I knew something was up, but I let it go. I figured the brother had plenty of time to haul his things over. Besides, he was probably scoping out exactly how much closet space he'd have to work with.

After finishing up the move, we stood on the balcony wrapped in each other's arms, taking in the glowing lights from the city's skyline. No words were spoken as we embraced in a kiss before hitting the shower and the bed.

Isaac and I had the perfect love affair. We'd spoil each other with the most elaborate gifts to the simplest of gestures. One year for his birthday I commissioned a charcoal drawing of him. When I first saw it, I thought it was just OK. But as I looked closer, I could see the artist had captured the essence of the man I loved, the one who recognizes my needs, walks with me as a partner, loves God and loves me dearly. At that moment, I felt a little piece of heaven.

Even though there was plenty of room, Isaac never officially moved in. Yes, he'd come over every day and stay late into the night, sometimes all night. But for whatever reason, he chose not to leave his mama's house.

It's funny, you know. When I met Isaac, a mutual friend of ours told me, "He'll make a good lover if you can get him out of his mother's house."

Like myself, Isaac was pretty much a loner. He had his close circle of friends and family. And even though he was outgoing and witty, he stayed to himself for the most part. Many people loved him because of his bubbly personality, but just as many hated him because they thought he was snobbish and stuck-up.

One day when he was at his mother's house, we were on the phone just talking about life and the people who mean the most to us.

He said, "I can name on one hand all of my true friends."

I chimed in, "I'm sure I can name at least two, Whitney and Madison."

He said, "Yep, you're right, add Jasmine and Apollo to the list and that's pretty much it."

Bells went off. Now I know Jasmine. Although I've never met her I had seen pictures of her. She was a beautiful girl who lived in Mobile with her husband and new baby. She sort of put you in mind of the R&B singer named Tamia. Jasmine was also friends with Whitney and Madison. But Apollo, I'd never heard of.

So by now my mind is racing and I'm asking myself, "Who is Apollo?"

So I said, "Oh, I've never heard you mention Apollo. Who is he?"

Isaac replied, "Oh, Apollo is my very best friend. We grew up together. His folks live around the corner from us."

He went on to tell me that Apollo had been living in Texas

for the past 10 years with his lover, but they had broken up so he came back home.

"Apollo and I go way back," he said. "We used to do every-thing together."

At this point, I'm trying to stay cool about this brand-new heavy in my man's life, especially since it was someone who was supposed to have been in his life all this time. I couldn't help but wonder why I had never even heard his name before.

So I said, "Oh, that's great, baby, so his name is Apollo. What's his last name?"

Isaac said, "Mason, Apollo Mason."

As we were talking on the phone I got up out of the bed, went to my desk, pulled out a pen and paper and jotted down the guy's name.

When Isaac and I got off the phone, I stared at the name that I'd just written down. I was trying to scan my brain's da-tabase to see if I could remember hearing that name anywhere before, but I came up empty. So I picked up the phone and dialed 411 for operator assistance. The phone rang twice.

"Thank you for using AT&T, how may I help you?"

"I'm trying to get a number and address for an Apollo Mason."

"What city and state?"

"Birmingham, Alabama."

She then gave me the information. I didn't know exactly why I'd made that call, but for some strange reason I knew it would become useful somewhere down the line.

As time went on I started noticing little things like Isaac leaving the apartment early and not answering his phone at night at his mother's place. He claimed he was asleep, but if his phone would ring while he was at my place, he didn't even let it ring three times before he was picking it up to say hello.

Not only had the quantity of time in our relationship changed, but so had the quality. After our regular Friday night movie, Isaac had gotten to the point where he would only come in and sit for a minute or so. He said he was getting sleepy and didn't want to disturb his mother by coming in too late.

There was a time when I would dial his number and he'd answer regardless of how late or early it was. Now I was lucky to get a returned call by noon the next day. And the excuses were always the same: "I was sleep," "my phone was off" or "it was in another room and I didn't hear it."

Therapy taught me that you can't change a person, but you can give them just enough rope to hang themselves. One Saturday morning after repeated calls to Isaac, I decided to dial Apollo's number that I had gotten over a month ago. The phone rang six or seven times before a guy finally picked up saying, "Hello."

I swallowed the lump in my throat and said, "Hello, may I please speak with Isaac?"

There was a long pause, but the tension was so thick you could cut it with a knife. After several moments of silence the voice on the other end calmly said, "I'm sorry you have the wrong number."

I tried to go on as if nothing had happened. The guy had told me I had the wrong number, so what else was I to do?

A month later I received a phone call. The voice on the other end said, "Lawayne?"

Trying to make out the voice I said, "Yes, this is he."

The guy went on to say, "You called my house a few weeks ago looking for Isaac, remember?"

My heart skipped a beat and I said, "Yes, I remember, but wait a minute, who is this?"

He said, "This is Apollo."

"Oh, Isaac's friend," I said.

With a little stank in his tone he said, "Yes, so what's going on with you and Isaac?"

In my cool, collected way, I replied, "Nothing much really, just loving and supporting each other like we always do."

"Oh yeah?!" he said. "Isaac told me that you guys broke up over a year ago before I met him."

Boom! Boom! Boom! That was the sound my heart was making from beating overtime. For a split second it felt like the breath was being sucked out of me.

I began questioning myself. Did I hear this man right?

Yes, I had.

Apollo went on to tell me that he and Isaac had been lovers for over a year. Plus, he said, Isaac told him that he and I didn't even communicate anymore.

While sitting on the side of the bed feeling sick to my stomach, all I could say was, "Well, man, this is all news to me."

He went on to tell me he started getting concerned the morning I called his house. That's when he admitted that Isaac was indeed there that day but refused to come to the phone. He also told me that he and Isaac had gone to an AIDS fundraising party which shocked me because parties, especially gay parties, were never Isaac's thing.

Apollo told me that at the party people began coming up to him asking, "Why are you with Lawayne's guy?"

He said at least 10 people asked him that. And I guess this morning he was calling to set the record straight.

Apollo and I were both shocked as we listened to stories from each other regarding Isaac for at least 2 hours. By the end of the conversation, I invited him to my house for lunch just to meet him. I had a thousand questions racing through my head. But I can't say I was mad . . . or even sad. The best way to describe what I was feeling was numb.

Before he got to my place I really didn't know what to expect. But based on our phone conversation, I didn't think there would be any drama. In a way, I felt proud of myself for having the courage to meet this man face to face. We were about to compare notes on the person that we had both been sleeping with for more than a year. When Apollo knocked on the door, I paused and took a deep breath before opening it. He was a tall, a golden-brown-colored man, not fat but thicker than I'd imagined him to be. Like me, he had a lazy eye and wore glasses. I remember saying to myself, "So *this* is who Isaac cheated on me for?"

We sat and talked for hours that day, comparing notes, dates, times and lies that Isaac had told both of us.

As it turns out, Apollo and I vaguely knew each other from church. I was a member of Covenant Community Church. It was a predominately white congregation that accepted all people. However, they had a large congregation of gay, lesbian, bisexual and transgendered people.

The service was a mixture of different religious influences from the pageantry of Catholicism with its candle lighting and communion, to the rhythm and soul of Pentecostals, complete with foot stomping and hand clapping. Apollo said he hadn't been to Covenant in a while, so I invited him to join me for worship on Sunday.

But until then, we spent the rest of the week comparing notes, never letting Isaac know that we finally figured out that he was playing both of us. I was hurt and angry, not to the point that I wanted to fight, but I did feel the need to get some kind of revenge.

After church, Apollo, along with my friends TJ and Andreas, came back to my place for lunch.

I've never been much of a cook, but TJ is a culinary wizard. In no time flat, he pulled together a garden salad filled with fresh greens, carrots, radishes, broccoli, feta and sourdough crisps. He marinated and pan seared four of the most mouthwatering steaks I'd ever tasted and baked four of the sweetest sweet potatoes God ever placed on this good green earth. Then he topped them off with butter and cinnamon.

The aroma coming from the kitchen was so intoxicating that when I finally got my plate I couldn't resist leaning over it to savor the homemade goodness. To enhance the experience we cheerfully sipped glasses of Cabernet Sauvignon as we reflected on Pastor J. R.'s message about allowing God to inspire our hearts with the assurance of love and peace.

After dinner, TJ mixed up a couple batches of margaritas while we all took turns telling our best jokes and quoting lines from our favorite movies.

Andreas had us cracking up with his rendition of Della Reese in *Harlem Nights*. He busted out with the part where Quick accuses Vera of stealing the money coming in from the prostitutes. He starts off by saying in his Vera voice, "Am I in charge of the girls?"

It quickly changes to them stepping outside for a fistfight, where Vera grits her teeth and says, "Oh, you wanna hit people with garbage cans?"

He finally winds up with, "There it is, Quick, go ahead and shoot me in my pinky toe."

Andreas had us rolling until TJ stepped right out of *The Color Purple* with, "You told Harpo to beat me?"

Then I chimed in with Florida Evans's, "Damn, damn, damn" from *Good Times*.

The evening was just fun, casual and drama free. It was so refreshing to just chill with my two best friends, and even though we didn't really know Apollo, he just seemed to fit right in.

As the sun started setting, Andreas remembered that his comedian friend Chris was performing at a club in Mountain Brook that night. We took a vote to see who all wanted to go, and everybody was in. It really didn't make sense to drive four separate cars, so we all decided to go in Andreas's Volvo station wagon.

TJ jokingly said, "Um, the perfect car for a 90-pound white woman from Mountain Brook."

In actuality, Andreas Pashley was a 6 foot 5 dark brown man who exuded intelligence, class and incredible humor. He was an educator and classically trained musician who toured Europe every summer singing Negro spirituals.

When we got to the club, the crowd was lily-white, but that was to be expected since it was in Mountain Brook, which is probably the richest zip code in Alabama. But the atmosphere was not at all stuffy. In fact, it was extremely relaxing and friendly.

By showtime we were already buzzing from the generous hands of the bartender, so every word out of the mouths of the comedians was hilarious. The improvisational show was set up just like Drew Carey's, *Whose Line Is It Anyway?*

From the time they started to the final curtain we were all laughing so hard our bellies ached. We left there completely entertained, fully intoxicated and not at all prepared for what was about to happen back at my condo.

It was just before midnight when we arrived back at my place, and Isaac was pulling out of the parking lot.

I didn't really know it was Isaac until we were actually

passing him because the lights on his SUV were so bright they nearly blinded me.

Apollo said Isaac had been blowing his phone up all afternoon and night. He had called me up a couple of times, but I never responded to his calls or texts.

Andreas pulled into a parking spot. Everybody was hype, wondering what was going to happen next. He and TJ offered to come in with me just in case Isaac wanted to act a fool, but I sent them on. We all assumed that Isaac had been driving around the parking lot all night and was shocked to see his secret lover's car parked outside my door.

I was nervous as I entered the apartment because I didn't know if he had been in and destroyed anything. I also didn't know if he was going to come back mad that I was hanging out with his lover. But something inside of me thought this was just what Isaac deserved.

"Let him sweat," I said, "just like he had me sweating when I found out about his yearlong love affair."

My heart was racing as I paced the floor. I wanted to talk to Isaac, but I didn't know what I would say. I'd been in situations similar to this before with Chazz and Chico, and they would always end up in a fistfight. But this was already different. I was proud of the way I'd been able to remain cool, calm and collected . . . to this point.

The phone rang. It was Isaac saying open the door, and I did. He rushed up the breezeway, pushed past me and slammed the door behind him.

With eyes filled with tears he asked, "What the hell is going on?"

I said, "*You* tell *me* what the hell is going on."

"Lawayne, I am so sorry I hurt you," he said.

Fighting back tears I asked him, "Why? Why are you cheating on me?"

He said he never meant for it happen, it just did.

I started asking him how they met, how long it had been going on and what did Apollo have that I didn't have, etc.

"You're both great guys," he said. "I am so sorry that I have hurt two awesome people."

I knew then that he had real feelings for Apollo and that I could lose Isaac for good. Even though I knew Apollo was not as good looking as me, nor did he have the charisma I had, I was still afraid that I may not be what Isaac wanted.

In my talks with Apollo we figured Isaac was using me for sex and him for money, romantic dinners and nights on the town.

Insecurity set in, and I was traveling down that same road I had been on so many times before. I was afraid he'd leave me, and I'd spend the rest of my life alone.

As I continued to ask Isaac why he cheated on me and if he was in love with Apollo, he pushed me and said, "You know what? I'm done with both of y'all."

Even though he had pushed me I couldn't hit him back. All I knew to do was hug him and beg him to please not go. "Let's work it out."

I wasn't thinking about the lessons of therapy or examples from the past. I literally held him all night, hoping he wouldn't leave me to go be with the man he had cheated on me with for over a year.

By the next morning we had decided we would stay together. Isaac told me that he loved me and was going to break it off with Apollo. Part of me believed it, but the other did not. A few days passed, and Isaac was MIA again.

He was always "asleep" or "running an errand for his mother" or "taking something to his grandfather."

Ordinarily, I wouldn't think anything of it, but since I found out about Apollo I was more than a little paranoid. I decided to drive by Isaac's house. It was about 9:30 Friday night, and when I turned onto his street I saw another vehicle approaching from the opposite direction.

I was not going to stop, but when the pearl-white Cadillac SUV pulled up in front of Isaac's house I knew it was Apollo, and I could see Isaac in the front seat.

Just as I was reaching his house, Isaac was getting out of the truck with a bag in his hands. I parked in the street, and he walked up to my car.

I was hurt and angry but calm enough to ask, "So what's up?"

Isaac said, "Lawayne, nothing is up. When Apollo called me, I told him I was about to go to CVS, but we needed to talk. He asked me if he could take me there so we could talk, and I said yeah. So on the way back I broke it off with him."

Back then I was so afraid of being alone I was willing to accept anything, even if it was a lie.

About a month later, I ran into a mutual friend of mine and Isaac's. Ironically, he had also been a friend of Chazz.

He and I started catching up, talking about what I'd been doing since Chazz died. I told him all about Chico and Isaac, and he told me he knew both of them.

He went on to tell me that he was having sex with Isaac, whenever and however he wanted and that Isaac was always hounding him to become his lover.

So there it was . . . again . . . staring me in my face . . . and I didn't have the strength or the courage to do anythin, about it all because I was too afraid of being alone. I was stuck in a holding pattern. Even though I knew the relationship wasn't going anywhere, I'd rather live with the lies than to live alone.

I was feeling all used up and thrown away. Even though I knew I needed to walk away, I couldn't.

My therapist and Gwen told me that it was probably the residual from when Mom left me at home alone for that one weekend when she went to Memphis to be with her lover.

Gwen asked me to start calling her whenever I got the urge to call Isaac. She also started me back to drawing the line down the center of the paper and writing all the good things on one side and all the negatives on the other.

She'd even quiz me verbally.

We'd go over scenario after scenario of what he'd done, how I'd responded to all of his lies and all of his cheating. We would talk about all of the disappointments that I'd endured, including his refusal to move in with me. My life was one big charade that had begun to weigh me down.

FIFTEEN

GOD WORKS IN MYSTERIOUS WAYS

CIVIL RIGHTS LEADER Fannie Lou Hamer coined the phrase: "I'm sick and tired of being sick and tired."

There was a hole in my heart that I knew only God could fill. After a series of bad relationships, drug addiction, sexual abuse and a host of other issues, I had finally reached a point where I too was sick and tired of being sick and tired any longer.

Even though God had delivered me from the bondage of crack cocaine, I was still suffering from a number of other issues, including separation anxiety, depression, guilt and problems sleeping.

I knew in my heart of hearts that if he could instantly deliver me from one of the most addictive drugs known to man, surely he could ease the years of heartache and disappointments that I had endured.

So I began to utter these words, "Save me, Lord. Forgive me of all my sins. Fill me with your Holy Spirit."

Every day, I would pray that God would renew my faith and take me back to that place where I met him 3 decades earlier. My soul cried out to God even as I was at work sending millions of dollars via wire transfer for AmSouth Bank. For weeks I sat at my desk in the computer room listening to gospel sermons and music from the time I began my shift until the time I finished working that day.

I'd pop in my earphones and listen to artists like Tramaine Hawkins sing, "What road should I take, what step should I make, oh Lord, what shall I do?"

And then I'd switch to Sandra Crouch singing, "You've been asking your friends, you've been asking your mother, you've been asking your lawyer, you've been asking the loan company, but you need to ask Jesus."

Every day my soul was crying out, "Do it for me, Lord. Revive my soul, Lord. Bless your name, Lord."

I put Psalm 37:4 to the test which says, "Delight yourself in the Lord and he will give you the desires of your heart."

My desire was for him to take control of the mess I had made of my life and to wrap his loving arms of protection around me.

All day, every day, with the words of my mouth and the meditation of my heart I'd say, "God, you're so awesome and worthy to be praised. You're the greatest, Lord. I give you my mind, my heart, I surrender everything to you."

Even as I walked to my car I was saying, "Bless your name, Lord."

While cleaning my house I was crying out, "Save me, Lord. Come into my life and forgive me of all my sins." The Bible says, "In all thy ways acknowledge him and he'll direct your path."

One afternoon while I was working at my desk, a feeling came over me that I had never felt before. It was kind of like that scene in *The Color Purple* where the choir is singing, *"God is trying to tell you something."* Or kind of like those Sunday mornings at Granddaddy's church when the deacons would sing, "I heard the voice of Jesus say come unto me and rest."

That day I heard that still small voice.

It was barely more than a whisper, but I instantly knew it was the voice of God. Right there, in the middle of dozens of computers, millions of checks and scores of people, I could feel the Holy Spirit.

A perfect peace had come upon me. I felt as if nothing could harm me anymore and down flowed tears of joy.

All alone in that small computer room my soul continually cried out. "Yay, Lord! Yay, Lord! Yay, Lord! Hallelujah!"

I tried to keep my cool, but I couldn't stop praising and worshiping God and neither did I want to. Being in his presence was better than anything I'd ever known.

God had heard my prayer and come into my life. Still I knew I wanted more of him. So I called Delois asking, "Are y'all having church tonight?"

"Nawl," she said. "But we're having Bible study."

I said, "No, I need more than that."

Delois told me I could come speak with the pastor, so I said OK.

But, of course, before I could leave work, everything that could go wrong did go wrong. We had all types of computer malfunctions. Payments wouldn't transmit, checks were not sorting correctly and the books weren't balancing. When I finally finished working it was about seven o'clock and Bible study started at 7:30.

I ran by the house to check on Mom.

She had cooked dinner so I woofed down a quick bite and jumped into the car to head to the church. But to my surprise, my car wouldn't start. It kept making that annoying *"eenngg, eenngg"* sound like the battery was about dead.

So I jumped in Mom's car. When I finally got on the road it was going on eight o'clock, and it takes a good 20 minutes to drive from my house to Bessemer even on the best of days.

I bobbed and weaved my way through the steady flow of I-20 traffic and navigated the streets of Bessemer.

As I pulled into the church parking lot I saw Delois's car and a handful of other cars that looked vaguely familiar. I quickly parked, jumped out of the car and ran to the door, but I couldn't get in because it was locked.

The neighborhood was not one of the safest in the city. In fact, the area was notorious for everything from homicides to burglaries to drug deals.

I kept knocking on the door, but they couldn't hear me. Just as I was about to give up, one of the brothers walked into the vestibule, heard me knocking and let me in. As I was taking a seat next to Lois, Bishop Capers was standing up to dismiss the congregation. In the middle of the benediction he paused and asked, "How many here are saved?"

A bunch of people raised their hands. He then asked, "How many here have the Holy Ghost?"

More hands went up.

From there he asked, "How many here *want* the Holy Ghost?"

I raised my hand and a few others raised theirs.

Then Bishop Capers said, "All who want the Holy Ghost come up here."

Before I was even halfway up the aisle the Holy Ghost had come upon me. I was speaking in tongues and praising and worshiping the Lord in a way that I had never done before.

I felt a power so strong and so pure inside of me. It was better than anything I had ever felt before. All at once, every one of my burdens seemed to melt away. For the first time in my life I had joy and perfect peace. I could literally feel God living inside of me. The Spirit of the Lord was all over the church. People were dancing and speaking in tongues and interpreting tongues. Like the rushing of a mighty wind, God filled the entire room.

After the Spirit had calmed, the pastor again started the benediction. It was not my intent to do it, but something told me to tell my cousin, "I want to join y'all's church."

Delois raised her hand, interrupting Bishop Capers with the news and a fresh anointing of the Holy Ghost filled the place again. I knew God was calling me into fellowship with New Beginnings Christian Church for a specific reason. I just didn't know what that reason was yet.

Finally we were dismissed, but I felt like a new creature. The Spirit of the Lord was all inside of me. I spoke in tongues all the way home.

When I got into the shower, the Holy Ghost was speaking directly to God from inside me. As I lay in my bed reading my Bible, it felt as if the Holy Ghost was being fed. It was as if the spirit inside of me was feasting on every word. Just like the Prophet Jeremiah said, it felt like an intense fire in my heart, trapped in my bones that I couldn't contain. The more I read the more powerful I felt. It seemed as if there wasn't anything I could not do.

When I arose the next morning I could still feel God's anointing all over me and deep inside of me. Even as I was getting dressed for work my soul was crying out to God, "Hallelujah! Thank you, Lord! Thank you, Lord!"

When I arrived at work, I tried to keep it to myself, but I couldn't. I had to tell somebody—anybody—everybody—what God had done for me. How he had filled me with the precious gift of the Holy Ghost. So I got up from my desk and started discretely visiting with coworkers in my office.

I began by walking up to them and asking, "Have you ever heard of the Holy Ghost?" Most of them would say, "Yes," and I'd say, "Well, I got it."

They all said with a smile, "Congratulations, that's good." Or they'd say, "Lawayne, I'm so happy for you."

After about the fifth or sixth person someone finally asked me, "What does it feel like?"

I had to stop and really think about it for a while. Then I realized that there really are no words to adequately describe exactly how it feels. But I tried to explain it in a way that I thought people might be able to at least get a glimpse of what I was feeling.

So I said, "Imagine your favorite artist is Michael Jackson, the greatest artist of all time." I then said, "Now, imagine you are on stage with him and he is performing in the largest concert the world has ever seen. Now, let's say it's being broadcast all over the planet on TV, radio and the Internet."

I then said, "Now, let's pretend Michael Jackson has sat you in a chair on stage with him, and he is singing a love song to you that you wrote especially for him to sing."

Then I upped it a notch and said, "The song that he's singing to you has turned out to be the best-selling record of all time."

By that time most were smiling or laughing and saying, "Wow!"

That's when I said, "Well, the Holy Ghost is even better than that."

I took that message to everyone in my office and even to some other areas of the building. But when I got to Cedric, a young man whom I had watched a few years back transform from one of Hells Angels to one of God's disciples, it became difficult to contain the spirit within me.

I felt so free. It was like I had overcome all of life's obstacles. I can only imagine what David must have felt when he talked about leaping over walls in the book of Psalms. The Holy Spirit was so strong that I didn't want to cause a scene in the office, so I asked Cedric to excuse me. I still remember him saying with a big grin on his face, "Man, that's all right." Everywhere I went I shared what God had done for me. Sometimes it was in words, sometimes it was through my smile and the new joy that flowed through me.

That Saturday night, a coworker was married at the Hilton Hotel in downtown Birmingham. It was a very grand affair with elaborate, floral decorations, lots of candles and beautiful people dressed in their finest clothing.

Entering the room I saw people in a way that I had never seen them before. People that I didn't even know were coming up to me inquiring about where they knew me from, but I didn't know them, and they didn't know me. I finally realized that it wasn't me that they recognized but the Holy Spirit that was now living inside me.

All night long there was a sweet spirit flowing through the room. The reception was just as spiritual. All of God's people were exuding the joy, peace, fullness and comfort that the Holy Ghost brings.

After dinner, the band started playing and the dancing began. The bartender uncorked bottles of the finest wines and alcohols and the libations began to flow.

I could have stayed and partook, but for some reason I didn't feel the need to. I was already on a natural high, so I quietly slipped out of the room, down the escalator and into the main lobby of the hotel. When I stepped onto the sidewalk the first thing I said was, "The Holy Ghost cut up tonight."

I had always heard that when you begin to walk by faith your whole mind changes. God and I had developed the kind of relationship where we actually spoke to each other. During one of our many conversations I asked him to show me my purpose in life. At the time I was working a good job at the bank, I also had a budding career as a voice-over artist. My voice had been heard in a number of productions from national radio ads to documentaries to corporate training materials to a radio soap opera.

Still, I knew God was calling me to do more. So I asked him with all sincerity, "What is it that you would have me to do, Lord?" I distinctly remember standing in my kitchen in front of the stove frying chicken in a black cast-iron skillet when God said to me, "I want you to speak my Word."

Without hesitation I replied out loud, "I'll speak your Word, Lord, I'll speak your Word." In that moment I began to praise God for choosing me to be his vessel. However, even though he chose me I knew that it was not about me but about what God could do through me.

I also knew that it didn't necessarily mean preaching to a congregation from a pulpit but simply by telling the stories of how God restored, renewed and redeemed my broken life. Scripture teaches us that in the last days God will pour out his spirit on all flesh. The Bible also says young men shall see visions and old men will dream dreams.

The vision God gave me was of an amazing outdoor festival right in the church's parking lot. It included a large concert with all types of religious bands and dancers. There was a health fair, art exhibits and a children's village with rides, face painting and puppets.

The next day I mentioned my vision to Delois, but I didn't elaborate on it. I think she may have said something like, "Boy, God may be trying to tell you something."

Then we changed the conversation to something else. About 3 days later, after Bible study, Bishop Capers and I were talking and he said, "You know, I'd like to have a big concert right out here in the parking lot."

My heart fluttered, and I told him I thought that was a great idea. I didn't tell him that God had just given me a vision of the same type of event. About a month later, Bishop Capers asked me if I'd be interested in planning an outdoor concert for sometime in the coming spring. With a big grin on my face I told him yes. That's when I described to him the vision God had given me. He seemed to be in awe and offered the church's full support, including manpower, money, whatever it took to make it a success.

During my days as a visual merchandiser several years ago, I had the opportunity to do some event planning. The store I worked for used to have an annual spring festival where they saluted a certain country. One year we saluted Spain, the next, India. So I had learned how to pull resources together to make a full-scale production with dinners, entertainers, even guest speakers. But I had never done anything on this scale outside of that organization.

The first thing I did was pray that God would direct my

path. I knew if this was going to be anything like what I had envisioned, I would need the support of the whole community, especially other churches. So I formulated a letter inviting them to join in on our efforts.

TJ and I took the letter to Kinko's to run off enough copies to mail out to the dozens of churches in the area. I wanted Isaac to go, but he was always too busy. When TJ and I got to the self-copier machine, someone had left us a gift that was obviously heaven sent.

It was a copy of a proposal to the city of Birmingham for an arts festival. The 1-inch thick document, complete with illustrations, gave step-by-step details on how to produce the exact kind of festival that I was putting together for the church. From that one document I learned how to go to the city of Bessemer and ask for basically anything I needed. The results were amazing.

The city gave us free use of an outdoor stage which was actually the flat bed that attaches to big rigs, but it suited our needs perfectly.

They even assured us they would beef up the number of officers patrolling the area on the day of the event. They hung dozens of banners on poles along the city streets to advertise the event.

January was winding down, and the event that we were officially calling *The Christian Gathering* was about 3 months away. That may seem like a long time, but in the grand scheme of things, it really wasn't.

Even though we had team leaders to cover every aspect of the event, everything ultimately fell on me. One of my flaws is that I have always been a bit of a perfectionist. So, of course, I wanted this festival to be as successful as the one God had shown me in the vision.

Eventually, I was micromanaging almost every part of the project. I was even making phone calls from work, running errands on my lunch breaks and visiting store owners in my spare time. My goal was to get them to donate whatever they could to our festival, be it goods or services.

I was constantly coordinating with each team leader to make sure everything was running as planned.

But when the commitments from the choirs and the dance teams seemed to be coming in slower than I thought they should, I began to really worry. So I started making personal appearances to their churches to get a solid agreement that they would be there and on time. Three weeks away from the Christian Gathering everything seemed to be falling into place. We had more than a dozen vendors signed up for the health fair. A local artist had agreed to bring his full exhibition of paintings, sculptures and other pieces. The list of choirs, soloist, rappers and dance troops had grown to nearly 20, enough for a full day of praise and worship. Members of the church and various restaurants had donated enough hamburgers, hot dogs and other foods to feed a small army.

The only thing that was missing was a sponsor for the children's village.

Everything was ordered, including the giant slide, bouncing balloon and all of the big blow-up toys that children love to jump up and down and roll around in.

The children's village was planned, but no one had stepped up to the plate with a check to pay for it. I was really starting to feel the pressure and was completely stressed out.

I know the church had told me not to worry about anything, but they still had not given me any money toward the equipment in the children's village. My body was getting weaker and weaker, and I had lost a lot of weight. But I attributed it to the rigorous schedule I had taken on with work and managing the Christian Gathering Project.

When I went for my regular doctor's appointment, he ordered routine blood work just to make sure everything was working properly.

I casually told my doctor about the event I was planning for my church. Something told me to ask if he had any little trinkets we could put in our goody bag as people walked through the health fair.

He said, "Sure, but I know a pharmaceutical representative who has worked on a similar project with a church in Atlanta. Would you mind if I give her your information?"

I said, "Of course, I wouldn't mind."

About an hour after I got home my phone rang. It was her.

She said, "Lawayne, it's Michelle Kirsey, Dr. Middlebrook told me about the community event with your church and we'd love to be a part."

She then went on to say, "Would it be OK if we donate a check for $1,500?"

Before the words were barely out of her mouth I began grinning and saying, "Yes! Yes! Yes! And thank you."

She promised to FedEx the check right away.

The Saturday before the Christian Gathering the event committee organized a neighborhood blitz. We met up at the church at ten o'clock that morning and canvassed the neighborhood, passing out flyers and knocking on doors, inviting everyone from the surrounding area to the festival.

After about 15 minutes, I was completely worn out. I had lost a lot of weight, and I was starting to look weak in my face. I was burning up with fever and had a slight cough. Everyone tried to get me to stop and go home, but I insisted on staying.

I tried to compensate by drinking extra water to hydrate, but the sweat kept pouring out and I became weaker and weaker. Finally about noon we had accomplished our mission.

I remember one of the church's sisters telling me, "You need to take yourself home and get in bed."

I got in the car and started the drive home, but it took all the strength I had not to pass out behind the wheel. I was so weary, weak and worn that it was all I could do to make it to Delois's house, which was a little more than halfway between my house and the church.

When I first got there I swung the car into her driveway, but all I could do was just sit there for several minutes while I regained my composure.

Finally I got the strength to walk to her screened-in porch and ring the doorbell. She opened the door and said, "Bruh Chiiry is you all right?"

My cousin was an educated woman who wrote and managed million-dollar grant projects. And although she could be articulate and sophisticated, she thoroughly enjoyed playing the role of a comedian.

Normally, I'd answer back with something just as silly like, "Yes, I is all right, cun Lois," but this time all I had the strength to do was stumble to her sofa and fall asleep. Eventually, I was awakened by the smell of something good cooking in the kitchen.

I hadn't had much of an appetite in weeks, but my body was now starving for food. However, even with an appetite, the smell of food had been sickening to me lately. But this time I was able to take little baby bites and get every bit of the meal into my system.

An hour after I'd eaten, I was still very weak, nervous and

now trembling from my lips to my hands to my feet. Delois asked, "Do you want to go to the hospital?"

"No, I'll be OK," I said.

I thought I had a bad case of the flu or something. I drove home, making sure that I didn't fall asleep or wander off into the wrong traffic lane.

Again I prayed, "Oh, Lord, please help me to get through this."

That Sunday I would have ordinarily gone to church, but I didn't. I was so worn out from the week and stressed out from all of the worrying. I was focused on making the Christian Gathering the huge success that God had already shown me it would be. But I couldn't help wondering if the money from the pharmaceutical company was really going to come through.

The next week I was only scheduled to work a couple of days at the bank. I had asked to be off Wednesday, Thursday and Friday because I figured I'd be trying to tie up loose ends. Everything seemed to be going as planned.

All of the groups had confirmed and all of the church members had been assigned their roles. The city confirmed that they were still going to honor their commitment.

The only thing that was not in place was the check.

By then, my body was obviously worn out. As I left work that Tuesday night, a couple of my coworkers were sitting outside on the smoker's bench. Passing by them I was so nauseated that I wanted to throw up right there in the trash can near where they were dumping their ashes. But I managed to bid them a good night and told them I'd see them next week. As I walked away and headed toward my car, I heard one say to the other, "Poor thing, he has lost so much weight."

Those words hurt like a punch to the gut because I knew

I looked the part of a person dying from AIDS. Their words continued to ring in my ears day and night, for weeks to come.

Wednesday morning I called Michelle at the pharmaceutical company.

"Michelle its Lawayne, I was just touching base with you about the check."

She said, "Oh my God, Lawayne, has it not come yet?"

"No," I said, "It hasn't come yet."

She apologized and said it was just an oversight, but she would FedEx it right out.

After I got off the phone with Michelle I breathed a sigh of relief and called the party rental store. With the date of the event quickly approaching I wanted to make sure all of the things I had ordered were still being held. And I wanted to reassure the store manager that I was coming to pay for it all. But until that check came, there was nothing I could do. Of course, I could have gone ahead and asked the church for the funds, but as the Word of God says, pride comes before every fall. Little did I know those words were starting to ring true in my own life.

Friday morning about nine o'clock I was still in my pajamas when the doorbell rang. When I got to the door, the FedEx man was headed back to his truck, but he had left an envelope on the porch with my name on it. I quickly ripped it open and there was the check for $1,500 made out to me.

In that moment as I held the check in my hand everything was made clear and I learned a lesson that day.

"Whenever God gives us something to do, he always gives us everything we need to do it."

That's what faith is all about . . . trusting in God and all of his promises.

I woke up about five o'clock Saturday morning completely

exhausted before I had even gotten up out of the bed. I lay there shaking, body aching and worrying if all of the choirs, dancers and other artists would actually show up for the event. Although my body was in its most feeble state, I knew I couldn't just lie there thinking about how sick and tired I was. I had to force myself up so that I could get to the church by eight o'clock. The first thing I did when I got out of bed was go upstairs to check on Mom. My body had become so weak that just making it up the few steps was a huge feat. By the time I finally reached her room I was out of breath and sweating profusely. I was so tired that I sat on her bed, which is something I seldom did.

As I asked, "Mom, how are you feeling?"

I could hear a wheeze in my voice and there was tightness in my chest that I hadn't noticed before. She told me I didn't look or sound good. I didn't feel well either, but I was going to go on to the church anyway. After all, this was the big day that God had given me in a vision 6 months ago, and now it was finally coming to fruition.

Even through the weakness and pain I couldn't help but think of how good it felt to know I was called to do a mission that was ordained by God.

After chatting with Mom for a few minutes, I made my way into the kitchen and put on a pot of coffee.

Coffee time was a favorite morning ritual of Mom and me. As it was brewing, I boiled some water to make instant oatmeal. Normally, I'd prepare us a more hearty breakfast with eggs, grits, toast and bacon or sausage. But today, I didn't have the energy. Plus I was too weak, too nervous and too excited about the Christian Gathering that was just moments away. After we finished breakfast, I eased into the bathroom to take a shower. My body was so worn that it was difficult to even take my pajamas off. Finally I got them off and just sat on the commode with the top down trying to catch my breath and stop shaking.

After the brief rest I reached over into the tub and turned on the water, being careful to adjust the temperature.

I was really having a bad day, and I didn't feel like fighting with water that was too hot or too cold. Getting into the shower, I had to face the fact that my physical health had swiftly deteriorated. I began praying out loud, "God, touch my body and give me the strength to stand and do your will."

I guess I was praying so loudly that Mom called out, "Son, are you OK?"

"Yes, ma'am, I'm OK," I said, but I knew I really wasn't.

I arrived at the church about a quarter to eight. The grounds were bustling with people hustling to get tents pitched and the stage equipment in place. The children's village which I had been so stressed out about was all coming to life.

Some of the crew members were already testing out the carousel and turning flips in the giant bouncing dome. The intoxicating aroma of BBQ ribs, chicken and sausages being smoked on the grill filled the air. The health fair and the art exhibition were also coming together nicely. And as far as I was concerned, just seeing the team work so well together and seeing how everything was falling into place had already made the day a success.

At ten o'clock the first choir was rocking the stage. The parking lot was already filled with happy people sitting in folding lawn chairs with umbrellas. They were singing along, clapping their hands and swaying to the beat.

Even though I was physically and emotionally drained I was floating on the fact that God had used me to bring people together for a day of praise, worship and celebration.

By noon, church members were telling me to go home because I was looking weaker and weaker by the moment. But I insisted on staying until the last group, which happened to be Christian rappers, left the stage. The group had driven all the way from Gadsden just be a part of our Christian Gathering. I wanted to thank every participant personally for making the day special.

The Christian Gathering was deemed a big success, but I would soon learn it had come with a huge price.

I wanted to stick around and help with the cleanup, but everyone insisted that I leave. My body was so worn out that I didn't really feel I had much choice. I needed to go home and lie down. I was hurting all over and needed to take something to ease the pain and hopefully help me to get a good night's sleep.

The rest of the weekend I remained restless. I didn't have an appetite for food, and all I could really stomach was maybe some cold Gatorade. When I was finally able to fall asleep, it was only for a short time. After about maybe an hour, I'd wake up drenched in sweat from my sleepwear to my bed sheets.

I was having the dreaded night sweats that I had heard so much talk about. I knew that was a classic symptom of AIDS. It made me more anxious to learn the results of my blood work that Doctor Middlebrook tested 2 weeks before.

Monday morning, Mom went to the doctor with me. It's a good thing she did because I was so weak I probably wouldn't have been able to keep the car on the road.

In the doctor's exam room, I tried sitting up on the side of the table, but I had to lie down because I felt so weak and irritated. My body was so cold that the nurse brought me four blankets to wrap up in.

Dr. Middlebrook finally made his way into the room. He sat on the short swivel stool, looked at me and Mom and said, "Looks like we have a very sick young man here."

I gasped for air.

"But we're going to put you on some medications, get you in the hospital for a few days and have you feeling all better in no time," he added.

"The hospital?" I asked, "Doc, how sick am I?"

He said, "You're very sick. The amount of HIV in your body is extremely high and the cells that help fight the disease are down to just three."

Even though I knew it, I felt compelled to ask, "Does that mean that I have AIDS?"

He said, "Yes."

My mom asked, "So he has AIDS?"

Dr. Middlebrook affirmed, "Yes, ma'am, he has AIDS."

Mom then asked, "Full-blown AIDS?"

The answer was the same. "Yes, ma'am."

For a brief moment I was in shock because with a T-cell count of three I didn't have anything to help me fight off the disease.

Plus any of my major organs could have shut down at any time. In actuality, I was well within the death zone.

I then asked Dr. Middlebrook if I had Pneumocystis pneumonia.

The answer was yes.

I knew Pneumocystis pneumonia was a life-threatening lung disease that commonly affects people with AIDS. I had watched it consume Cheryl and Chazz and hundreds more friends and loved ones.

After 10 years of living with HIV and watching scores of friends and loved ones die from AIDS it had finally hit home.

While sitting in the chair next to my mother, I held back my own tears as I wiped away the tears rolling down her face.

From the day I entered the hospital, I was poked, prodded, injected and I believe everything else that could possibly be done to a person was done to me. I was constantly given antibiotics, x-rays, CAT scans and dozens of blood tests. They even hammered a nail-like needle into my tailbone to do a bone marrow biopsy, trying to determine if I had tuberculosis, but that test, thankfully, came back negative.

After about 6 weeks my doctor released me from the hospital, but I was still a very sick man. He put me on steroids to help repair damage done to my lungs by the Pneumocystis pneumonia.

Since I'd become ill, I had lost about 50 pounds and was extremely frail. On the day I left the hospital, Dr. Middlebrook told Mom to let me eat anything I wanted.

He said, "If he wants to eat two hamburgers, French fries and a large shake let him have it." His main concern was to get weight back on me.

I never should have heard those words come out of his mouth because I took him literally.

Of course, I knew I needed to gain my weight back because I had lost both body fat and a whole lot of muscle. But because of my own vanity I didn't want to gain as much weight as I did. Within a few weeks I started packing on the pounds. The steroids kept me hungry to the point that I could eat a full pancake breakfast with sausage and eggs and be hungry again 30 minutes later.

Even though I was better, my doctor was still trying to find the right combination of drug therapy to stop the progression of HIV in my body. The first combination he tried me on made me have the craziest dreams.

They were so vivid that they seemed real. In one dream

I was running deep in the jungles of Africa, then I was captured and forced to have wild unprohibited sex with native warriors.

In another I was flying high over Niagara Falls and suddenly decided to take a nosedive directly into the icy-cold falls.

Even though the water was as cold as ice, my body stayed warm and everything seemed peaceful.

Aside from the disturbing dreams I was also continuously having those terrible night sweats. They were part of the side effects that went along with the medication. But these were far worse than the ones I was having before I went into the hospital.

Like clockwork, they began in the latter part of the day just before sundown. They would last all night into the early-morning hours when the sun was coming up. That made getting a good night's sleep virtually impossible because I was constantly up and down changing my pj's and bed linens.

It was so exhausting that I whispered to God, "Lord, unless you have something for me to do, close my eyes and take me on home to be with you. But if you have something for me to do I need you to raise me up and give me the strength to do it."

The next week, Doctor Middlebrook put me on another cocktail that actually worked without all the side effects. As I began feeling better, my doctor asked me if I was ready to go back to work. My heart sank. I still remembered my last day at AmSouth and what my coworker said as I was leaving the building for the last time. *"Poor thing, he has lost so much weight."*

I knew that day I was too embarrassed and humiliated to ever go back to work there.

I quickly told Dr. Middlebrook, "No, I can't go back. It

makes me nervous just thinking about having to go back into that environment."

He asked, "Well, what do you want to do then?"

I quickly said, "I'd like to go to school."

"Well, go to school then," he said. "What are you going to study?"

I said, "Broadcast journalism."

He replied, "Well, good for you."

That day, instead of going home to die, I went home to finally start living life.

SIXTEEN

GOD EQUIPS THE CALLED

WHEN I ACCEPTED God's call to speak his Word I knew I was opening myself up for him to use me as he saw fit.

Even before I enrolled at Jefferson State Community College, Kym's sister, CC, asked me to be part of a Black History program at Miles College. Miles is the only school in Birmingham that's part of the historically Black college and university system. At the time, CC was a student in the department of social work. She was also known for developing elaborate productions with the communications and theater departments.

This particular program that she asked me to be a part of was called *Poetry in Motion*. CC had the outstanding talent and expertise of her fellow students and faculty at her fingertips. So when she asked me to participate, I was taken by surprise. I asked, "Why do you want *me* on the program?" She said, "Because I know you'll bring your A-Game, and you will motivate the others to do their best."

I was humbled by her faith in me. Sure I had done voice-over work on a number of productions for companies and corporations like the Miami Heat, the New Jersey Nets and numerous financial institutions. I had also voiced corporate training materials, campaign ads, documentaries, even video games. In fact, I was even blessed to have been cast in the leading male role of a radio drama called *Bodylove*. It was a real soap opera with all the drama of shows like *General Hospital, One Life to Live* and *Days of Our Lives*. Many people even compared *Bodylove* with the popular radio drama *It's Your World,* from Tom Joyner's *Morning Show*. Mom listened to *It's Your World* every day.

BodyLove mixed melodrama with real health issues plaguing communities of color at the time. Ironically, my character was the abusive, alcoholic husband and father who was eventually redeemed and became a pillar of the community. I guess that was a real example of art imitating life.

The show was produced by the University of Alabama at Birmingham and Boutwell Studios. It ran for about 3 years on radio stations across the Southeastern U.S. But when funding ended so did *BodyLove*.

It's kind of funny how I ended up doing voice-over work. It all started at a backyard BBQ party at TJ's house. I struck up a conversation with a neighbor, and it came up that he was a DJ. I thought that was a pretty cool job so I asked if he enjoyed the work. He said, "Being a DJ is OK, but I really like when I get to do voice-over work."

I asked, "Voice-over work? What is that?" He went on to tell me it could be anything using his voice, from simple station promos to commercials. Instantly I had that "aha!"

moment because that's something I'd always wanted to do. So I jokingly asked the redheaded, fair-skinned, 20-year-old named Paul, "How can a 'brutha' break into the business?"

We laughed for a minute, and then he told me he had taken Marie Prater's voice-over class at Boutwell Studios. He continued, "Yeah, she usually does them about twice a year." He then went on to tell me after he took her class, it gave him the confidence and tools he needed to start promoting his talents.

The next day I called Boutwell Studios and inquired about the classes. The receptionist told me that Marie actually had a class starting in about 2 weeks, but it was filling up fast. So I immediately paid my money and signed up. The class met at 6 p.m. twice a week for 3 weeks.

The night of the first class was the first time I had been in a recording studio in years. It took me back to my elementary school days when we recorded the show about preventing child abuse at Alabama Public Radio. Since then, I had been to plenty of studio sessions to watch Herman record for himself and a number of bands and singers. The voice-over class was meeting in Studio-D. It was a dimly lit room with 20 chairs in a semicircle position.

With the exception of an older female, I was the only other black person to help fill those chairs. Midway through the first night Marie said, "We're going to give everybody a chance to go into the sound booth and record something." My heart skipped a beat.

"Now don't be nervous," she said.

I'm thinking, *Too late. I'm already nervous.*

She continued, "This won't hurt a bit."

While flipping through a large binder, she said, "You can record something you wrote or you can read one of these commercials that have already been recorded here at Boutwell."

Many of the students were sort of squirming in their seats. I don't think any of us expected to be in the recording booth on the very first night. I was already feeling insecure because I was the only black guy in the class, plus I was probably the youngest person in the room.

As I sat there listening to one great voice after another, I started feeling more intimidated. Suddenly, I heard a small voice somewhere inside of me, and I knew it was God telling me to not to be discouraged. He was saying, "This is the moment you have been waiting for. This is what you have been dreaming of. Trust me, I got you."

Moments later it was my turn to enter the booth, so I took a deep breath and said a simple prayer.

"Lord, I pray that you will speak through me and that this audience will be amazed."

When I entered the booth, it was as if I had a new boldness. I decided to use something I was comfortable with; a piece I had done when I commentated the Chazz Fashion Review. With a newfound energy and inner support I began, *"It's more than just a fashion show; it's a fashion extravaganza . . ."*

After I finished, I received a big applause and high fives. Of course, I thanked my classmates for their kindness, but I chalked it up as common courtesy. The rich voices and personalities in the room kept me mesmerized as the class continued. In the end, we were all critiqued by Marie and nationally renowned voice-over artist Ken Osbourn. Ken is a mature white man who is legally blind. But he has the incredible ability to do things with his voice that I can only dream of doing. Most people have heard Ken's clear crisp baritone voice on hundreds of national television and radio commercials and many dramatic movie trailers.

. . . So imagine the rush I got when at the end of the night Ken told the crowd, "Lawayne has the voice we're looking for."

My heart stopped. I asked myself, did this man say what I think he just said? All I could think was that only God could have done that.

A week after the class ended I received a phone call from a person with a familiar cheery voice.

"Lawayne, it's Jill at Boutwell. Greg asked me to call to see if you can come in for an audition."

My knees were shaking, and I had a smile a mile wide as I said, "Sure, I can!"

When I got there, Greg handed me a script for an automobile marketing firm, saying, "Read this over and we'll go into the booth in a minute."

I read it a few times, and then I prayed. "God, I pray that you will speak through me and that the people will be amazed."

Inside the studio, the engineer adjusted my microphone and played a little bit of the music that would lay under my voice. It was a jazz piece with lots of class. I put on my headphones and took a deep breath and out came a deep, rich, sultry voice that I instantly knew must have come from God.

The producer loved what he heard, and before long I was getting more calls from Boutwell. It was the beginning of a long lasting relationship that I've always cherished.

Although I had done tons of studio work, I seldom had the opportunity to perform in front of a live audience. Without even considering the fact that I was still battling aches and pains associated with complications from AIDS, I didn't let it stop me. I told CC that I'd do the *Poetry in Motion* program performing the poem Maya Angelou wrote and performed for President Bill Clinton's first inauguration. It's called *On* the Pulse of Morning. When I heard her recite it, I instantly felt she was speaking to something deep within my soul. It actually inspired me to reexamine my own life and strive for everything I ever dreamed of. But obviously, I had lapses of initiative along the way.

Weeks before the production I began studying. I started dissecting every word, making sure I was able to understand what they meant and how they made me feel. By the day of the event I was so hyped that I couldn't relax. So I went ahead and drove across town early to the school, nestled in the residential community of Fairfield.

Driving onto the campus I could see dozens of students carrying book bags and sporting Walkman stereos with headphones in their ears. Just knowing that I was among young people like my friend CC who were doing amazing things, my adrenaline began working overtime.

Then I realized I was in the midst of academia at its finest. It was a place I admired and wanted to be. As I entered Brown Hall auditorium, there were only a handful of students in a room that could hold a few hundred. Most of them were doing final performance rehearsals.

Kym and CC's mother, Mrs. Black, were sitting in the hard wooden theater-style folding seats. Chatting for a while with Mrs. Black, my nerves began to calm. She told me in her soft angelic voice, "I have always enjoyed hearing you speak."

Then with her flirtatious, girlish grin, she said, "In fact, I could sit and listen to you all day with your cute self." We both laughed. She always had something fun and encouraging to say. And it worked because after spending time with her I couldn't wait to get up on that stage.

Besides, after days of practice I had reached a level where I wasn't only reciting the poem, I had *become* the poem. I was so connected to *On the Pulse of Morning* that I started believing I could actually achieve everything Ms. Angelou was saying in the piece.

I was especially moved by the lines, "Each new hour holds new chances for new beginnings . . . Do not be wedded forever to fear . . . Give birth again to the dream."

I began realizing that there was so much more to me and that I was not fully living up to God's expectations for my life. Approaching the stage, I realized how much the audience had swollen from just a few people to hundreds of students, faculty and guests. When I finished the poem and began to leave the podium, thunderous applause filled the room. The program was so successful that the school's president wanted to take *Poetry in Motion* around to all of the secondary schools in the area. And even though I was not part of the Miles student body, I was invited to travel with the show.

I had considered attending Miles, but like so many other HBCUs, the high cost of tuition was beyond what I could possibly afford. That's part of why I decided to take classes at Jefferson State Community College. Jeff State was known for its on-air radio station and live television capabilities. It had earned the reputation of being one of the best broadcast journalism schools in the state. Right after I told Dr. Middlebrook I wanted to go back to school, I applied for a Pell grant to help pay my way. Unfortunately, after answering hundreds of questions on several pages of the application, I was still turned down. They said I had exhausted my funds when I started college right out of high school and flunked out miserably. I did, however, get a student loan with a low interest rate to get me through the first year.

From the day I decided to go back to college for broadcast journalism, I began praying that God would help me keep up with the rigorous routine. On my first day at Jeff State I was as nervous as a rooster in a henhouse. I knew I looked different because at 40 I was much older than the average student fresh out of high school. A couple of them even asked if I was the professor.

Unlike the time I enrolled in college years before, this time I was determined to excel in everything I set out to do. And I wasn't going to let lovers or drugs get in my way. I felt like I finally had the opportunity to redeem myself.

Besides, now that I was back in school, there was no way I was going to let my young classmates outshine me. I developed excellent study habits and did all of my assignments on time. Math had always been my Achilles' heel. But I quickly found out that if I studied hard and saw my tutor on a regular basis I excelled in those classes too.

I was a man on a mission and *nothing* was going to stop me from achieving my goal. I finished the semester with all As. But the mistakes of the past were always going to be part of my future.

Between semesters, I had a doctor's appointment. My lab work showed that the AIDS medication I was taking was having an adverse reaction on my kidneys.

Dr. Middlebrook decided to take me off of one of the meds and tried me on a different drug. Unfortunately, the side effects to the new medicines were unbearable. The night sweats returned, and again they were so bad that I would wake up several times during the night soaking wet from my pj's to my bed linen. My doctor thought the side effects would go away after about a week or so, but they did not. It took weeks before he found another drug therapy that my body could tolerate.

Unfortunately, I had to sit out the fall session. When I tried to enroll in classes that spring, I was denied. The admissions office said I had reneged on my student loan by sitting out a semester. They said the only way I could enroll would be to pay the balance of my student loan or pay the tuition myself. Now that I was on disability, there was no way I could afford to pay my way through college.

It was clear to me now what my mother meant when she had told me time after time before she got sick, "Son, go to school while I can help you."

Again, stress and anxiety set in. So I began to pray and utilize some of the tools I had learned through therapy to deal with situations like this. I found myself getting in my car, rolling down the windows, opening the sunroof and driving down First Avenue North until I reached East Lake Park. Sitting on top of a picnic table, I focused on a flock of ducks effortlessly gliding across the lake. A warm breeze gently blew against my back, and all of my senses seemed to heighten.

It took me back to those days when I was a boy, playing in the creek behind Poppa Gray's house. I could distinctly hear the sounds of the birds singing and the frogs croaking along the water's edge. And as I gazed up into the sky I saw the leaves on the trees waving to the sun and a still small voice whispered to my heart that with God's help, everything was going to be all right.

I got up off that bench and drove to Jefferson State to tell my advisor, Ray Edwards, why I wouldn't be coming back to school. I had the utmost respect for Mr. Edwards. He was a broadcast pioneer and had taught hundreds of professionals who were working in the field. He was familiar with some of my voice-over work, and I knew he was expecting great things from me.

I found him in his office sitting at his desk filled with papers. While on the phone, he motioned for me to come on in and have a seat. A stack of school newspapers that he had collected over the years rested on a file cabinet and a poster of "Rocking Ray the DJ," his alias, was tacked to the wall among a collage of posters, newspaper clippings and other memorabilia.

Mr. Edwards was an upbeat gentle soul. His short statue, silver hair and charisma made him a dead ringer for Mickey Rooney. After hanging up the phone he turned to me with a smile on his face and a voice filled with cheer.

"Welcome back, sir."

I said, "It's good to see you too, sir, but I have some bad news."

Because of my respect for Mr. Edwards I wanted him to understand that I was not just quitting school. I explained to him that because of my medical and student loan problems, the financial aid office wouldn't allow me to register this semester.

With a surprised look on his face I remember him asking, "Really? Are you better now?"

I said, "Yes, still a little weak but much, much better."

That's when he said, "Well, I'll tell you what. Don't worry about it. I'll give you a scholarship."

My eyes bucked wide, my mouth flew open and all I could say was "Huh?"

He smiled and said, "Yeah, we'll pay all of your tuition and fees."

I wanted to be sure I was hearing him correctly so I asked, "Are you serious?"

"Sure," he said. "You are my most dedicated student."

Mr. Edwards rambled through his file cabinet and pulled out a scholarship application. He filled it out, signed it, and asked me to sign it and take it to the registrar's office.

Still shocked, I said, "Oh my God, Mr. Edwards, thank you so much. I promise one day I'll make you proud."

He laughed and said, "What are you talking about? You're already doing that. You are my best student, and you're an excellent example for the rest of the class."

We shook hands and I backed out of his office thanking him over and over.

Still laughing he said, "You better go ahead and get that turned in."

A never-ending friendship was born that day.

On the way to the registrar's office all I could say was, "Thank you, Lord!"

My resolve to succeed was at its greatest. Just as I had willed myself to beat my crack addiction, I also willed myself to succeed in college. I wanted to learn everything I could. I took every class available on the processes of radio and television production. That included how to write news, operate cameras and other television equipment. I also learned the ins and outs of running a radio station.

As part of my training I had to do a live on-air radio show twice a week. The first day I was to go on the air was more than I ever bargained for. I was eating breakfast and passively watching TV when I heard Tom Brokaw announce breaking news.

"A plane has crashed into the World Trade Center."

News reports were predicting that it was equipment or pilot error. Then as I sat there watching *The Today Show*, waiting to hear more information, I actually saw a second plane crash into the second tower.

Tom Brokaw's coverage now included the words, *"A terrorist act of war against this country."*

I was glued to the TV, anxious and wondering what was really happening.

I finally pulled myself away, got dressed, grabbed my keys,

jumped in my car and immediately turned on the radio. That's when I heard that a plane had hit the Pentagon and another had crashed in a field in Shanksville, Pennsylvania.

Then the first tower of the World Trade Center collapsed.

A few minutes later it was announced that the second tower had collapsed.

While parking the car and walking into the building, I couldn't help but wonder what was next. I had never seen what the news reporters were now calling acts of terror.

The halls which were usually bustling with students hurrying to and from class were suddenly quiet and calm, but once I entered the radio station all hell had broken out. The soft rock programming was replaced with live coverage of the unprecedented turn of events. Phones were ringing, faxes were constantly coming in and the senior student radio announcers were scrambling to get the latest news of the attacks on the air.

Instead of going on the air, I spent 9/11/01 making phone calls, trying to book local experts on war and terror to do live interviews. In between calls, I was passing wire copy to the announcers.

I didn't actually make my radio debut until a week later, but the experience I received on 9/11 helped me to understand the intensity and demands of live breaking news.

That one intense event made me more determined and dedicated to learning my craft. I began reading news publications every day just to stay abreast of what was happening in the world.

After class, I'd go home, cook, take my mother to her doctor or hair appointments, clean the house, and then submerge myself in my books and notes from class. The learning and experience just kept coming.

After I delivered my first presentation in Speech 101, the

instructor approached me with a simple question. "You do know we have a speech team here at Jefferson State, right?"

"Yes, sir," I said. "It's something I've been considering but never knew how to go about it."

"Well, you just go right upstairs and speak with Dr. Janice Stuckey," he said. "She's the director of Speech Communications. Tell her I sent you."

Gratefully, I said, "Thank you, sir, I'll do that."

Quite frankly, I had been hesitant about approaching Dr. Stuckey simply because of her name. I thought a name like Stuckey had to belong to one of those old-school English professors. If that was the case, I didn't think she would be able to relate to a 40-year-old black man, full of confidence, but still struggling to reach the peak of his own abilities.

When I finally met Dr. Stuckey, she was nothing like I expected. She was a beautiful blond-headed woman, at least 3 or 4 years younger than I. Dr. Stuckey had swagger, class and a realness about her that helped put me at ease. Her tiny office was filled with hundreds of books from all genres of literature. They included adult fiction, science and technology, religion and self-help manuals.

Dr. Stuckey went on to tell me all about how the forensics speech team did everything from platform to interpretive speaking. "That includes informative, persuasive, even after-dinner speeches. We also do prose, poetry, dramatic interpretation and program of oral interpretation," she said. "Of course, we do impromptu and occasionally someone will do critical analysis." She was explaining it all so fast I could hardly take it all in.

Each team event was limited to a 10-minute time frame. Within that time span, contestants had to give a brief tease of the piece, an introduction explaining the social significance of the presentation, and the rest of the time was to complete the program.

Even though diction was part of the judging criteria, it was only a small part. The heart of forensic speech is how well you can effectively communicate the story to your audience. It is also based on the correct amount of eye contact, body language and the proper display of emotions.

Forensic speech is an academic sport, and I was hooked from my very first tournament at Berry College in Rome, Georgia. A certain magic happened when Christine Goss, our assistant coach, pulled the 12-passenger rental van carrying our 10 team members into the parking lot. Other teams were stepping off of vans wearing business attire prepared to battle it out in dozens of classrooms. The more tournaments we attended I couldn't stop thinking about the big picture. These kids could be at a football stadium cheering their teams on to victory. But dang! They have chosen to give up their weekends to compete in their own academic sport.

Even though I was usually one of the oldest students competing, I fit right in. I think it helped to keep me young and determined to be the best.

Forensics taught me more about storytelling than all of my writing classes combined. Imagine having to condense a story from a 300-page novel down to a 10-minute presentation. That's what you learn to do in forensics.

My favorite event is the Program of Oral Interpretation, or POI. It combines various genres of literature, like prose, drama and poetry, into one story. The event is so versatile that the topics can range from extremely humorous to extremely serious and sensitive. I took every opportunity to explore those possibilities.

In one of my POI presentations, I told the story of the

Tuskegee syphilis experiment. That's where the U.S. government systematically failed to treat hundreds of poor black sharecroppers from Macon County, Alabama, who had syphilis. For 40 years, the men were never told they had the disease, nor were they ever treated for it. Instead, they were told they were being treated for "bad blood."

To tell the sobering story, I used scenes from the movie *Miss Evers' Boys* combined with excerpts from President Bill Clinton's formal apology on behalf of the U.S. government. It read in part:

"The United States government did something that was wrong, deeply, profoundly, morally wrong. It was an outrage to our commitment to integrity and equality for all our citizens. We can end the silence. We can stop turning our heads away. We can look at you in the eye and finally say on behalf of the American people what the United States government did was shameful, and I am sorry."

Another of my POIs that garnered national honors examined the old African American debate of good hair versus bad hair. Logic would suggest that good hair is simply healthy hair. But as I demonstrated through prose, poetry and drama, good hair can be far more complicated for black women who often equate it with long silky hair. As a result, millions of black women spend countless hours and millions of dollars using chemical relaxers and weaves to make their hair straighter and longer. Mom even started having weave put into her hair after her brain surgery years ago. She wanted to thicken up the small patch that grew back thinly where they cut into her scalp.

As a member of Jeff State's Speech Team, I was able to see a huge chunk of the country. We traveled from Alabama to Florida to Illinois to Oregon and a dozen states in between.

Although we were a 2-year school, we primarily competed against larger, 4-year institutions like the University of Alabama, William & Mary University, Morehouse College and Tennessee State University.

Janice and Christine would often have team meetings at their homes where we'd practice our craft over salad and lasagna. We became a family and developed friendships that remain to this day. Sometimes we would stay at their homes late into the night working on our delivery. Ultimately, that persistence paid off. I made it into the final rounds of numerous competitions. That meant I was also bringing home medals for our team. My greatest accomplishments came when I won gold, silver and bronze at the Phi Rho Pi National Championships.

Forensics helped to hone my communications and critical thinking skills. It also taught me how to dissect a subject and quickly put it into a story form that was easily digestible for the listener.

By the time I began my internship at Birmingham's ABC 33/40 television station, I was full of confidence. Tracy Bynum was the station's internship coordinator. She also produced the five and six o'clock evening newscasts. Tracy had been in the news business for years. Her passion for her work was infectious. She had a way of helping the interns to relax and be serious without becoming cocky. During our orientation, Tracy posed a funny yet serious question to the half dozen of us in the program.

"What is the most embarrassing thing that has ever happened to you?"

Of course, there were many answers. But Tracy confessed that mine was by far one of the most original she had heard in her entire career.

The story I told was true.

One day while traveling from Memphis to Birmingham I had to do the "number two" so badly, but there wasn't a restroom anywhere in sight. It had gotten to the point where I was squeezing my cheeks, sweating and praying that I would make it to a facility. Finally the urge was so strong I had to pull over or risk messing everything up. So I pulled off the interstate onto a country dirt road, shielded myself from view with the car door and squatted.

I ended up staring into the eyes of a bullfrog that must have been wondering what the heck I was doing in his house. Before he could croak, I had wiped up with my T-shirt and left it there with him. After making my way to the first service station, I washed up, changed my shorts and continued my journey to Birmingham.

Tracy said the purpose of the exercise was to show all of us that everyone has a story to tell. The important thing is to gain their trust and to tell their story with dignity.

That semester, I worked in nearly every position in the news department, from operating studio cameras, to doing research for producers. But my biggest focus was spending time with reporters. At last I was a step closer to fulfilling my childhood dream. Whenever the reporters went out on assignment, I'd tag along, write my own story, call Tracy for an edit and do a stand-up for my demo tape.

I instantly developed an appreciation for the access to people, places and things given to reporters. During that one semester I had covered dozens of stories from the death of Pope John Paul II to a mountain lion on the outskirts of Birmingham. But the infamous trial of former HealthSouth Corporation CEO Richard Scrushy was a doozy.

The HealthSouth founder had been charged with nearly

3 dozen counts of fraud, reporting false corporate earnings and lying to shareholders. The trial lasted for months, and we spent numerous hours in the courthouse covering all the details. The court proceedings would usually wrap up in time for a live report on the five and six o'clock newscasts. But this particular day, testimony seemed to never end. Kevin, the reporter I was with, was in constant communication with the studio.

He called to tell Tracy, "This thing doesn't seem to be wrapping up anytime soon. I may not have a bite from anybody for my package or VO."

Then five o'clock came, and the judge was still hearing testimony. Kevin did a stand-up in front of the courthouse, giving highlights of what was happening in the courtroom. But the weather was terrible. It was so rainy and windy that his umbrella blew away while he was on the air.

After the five o'clock newscast didn't work as planned, Tracy was still hoping for at least a bite from the attorneys for the six o'clock report.

"Hang in there," she said. "They will probably wrap up in a minute."

Court eventually did wrap up about a quarter to six, but none of the witnesses spoke with the media. The best we could hope for was something from the attorneys. Finally, attorneys for both sides came out, but they weren't talking. After standing in the dark, and the cold rain, all we got was "no comment."

I was chilled, wet and hungry. My nose was runny, and I had a headache that wouldn't let up. I thought maybe I should reconsider news reporting as a career because I was not feeling standing out in the cold and rain for just a "no comment." But in the news business, every day is different. The next day I was in the state capitol talking with lawmakers about the need for mandatory pre-k in Alabama. I had fallen in love with chasing news all over again.

By the time my internship ended, I had a polished demo tape that I could show prospective employers. It had a variety of news packages and stand-ups that I had produced. Tracy said she was so impressed with my work ethic that she wanted the news director to offer me a position with the station. Of course, that would have been a feat because landing a first job in a major TV market like Birmingham is next to impossible.

She felt so strongly about my potential that she told Mr. Edwards if I had done maybe two internships I possibly could have had a real chance of getting hired. And what do you know—Mr. Edwards said he changed the program's internship requirements from 1 year to 2.

Finally, graduation day was within reach. I had been inducted into Phi Theta Kappa Honor Society and won three national forensic speech championships. Life was looking promising. The afternoon of the commencement exercise it felt as if I was floating on air. Mom, Aunt Jean, my dad's sisters, Aunts Katie and Oshie Mae, Isaac and many more of my family and friends were cheering me on as I walked across the stage. I was excited about them seeing me in my cap and gown, complete with honor cords. But I couldn't stop reflecting on a lesson I learned when I was organizing the festival for the church.

That lesson is . . . Whenever God gives you something to do, he'll give you everything you need to do it. All we have to do is put our faith into action.

SEVENTEEN

THE BEST IS YET TO COME

"WE'VE COME THIS Far By Faith" is a song that I've been singing since I was a little boy. Granddaddy used to sing it, Mama used to sing it and it's a Sunday morning staple of churches everywhere. Even though I had heard the words nearly all of my life, I have yet to fully appreciate their meaning.

The morning after graduation I was in the kitchen preparing breakfast. I put on the coffee, scrambled the eggs and was waiting for Mom to make her way into the kitchen to give the final approval of my grits. Unlike my granddaddy and Mom, my grits were always too lumpy, too soupy or just not seasoned right.

It took her a while to make it in because she was using her hemi-cane. A full-size walker would have given more stability, but because her left arm was constricted, the hemi-cane was a better fit.

I called out, "Mama, don't be dragging your foot. Pick it up."

She said, "I'm picking up my foot."

Mom was feeling good that day and quickly OK'd my grits.

"For real, Mama?"

"Yes," she said. "They look perfect."

Smiling, I said, "Well, I hope they taste as good as they look."

When she got to the table I nervously watched to make sure she didn't miss the chair. After about her sixth stroke her body had weakened significantly and she started falling more frequently.

"Mama, are you all right?" I asked.

Even though her mouth was slightly twisted her speech remained almost perfect.

"Yes, I'm fine," she said.

Yes, she was fine that time, but it was getting to the point where I was afraid to leave her home alone for fear of her falling. I had already come in a couple of times to find her on the floor. She asked me to lead us in grace.

"Lord, thank you for being God, the Creator of all things. Thank you for watching over us as we slept and slumbered through the night. We praise you for waking us up this morning. And we thank you for giving us a reasonable portion of health and strength. And thank you, Lord, for this food that you have provided. We pray that it will go toward the nourishment of our bodies. In Jesus' name we pray, amen."

"Son, that was a mighty fine prayer," Mama said.

Breakfast was usually when we shared some of our most intimate thoughts. That day the conversation started with Mom saying, "Son, I am so proud of you."

"Me?" I questioned.

"Yes," she replied. "I'm proud of you for having the courage to reach for your dream. But not only did you reach for it, you grabbed it."

Looking at that woman who has always been my tower of strength, I said, "Mama, do you know what gave me that courage?"

"God?" was her reply.

"Oh no doubt, God," I agreed. "But do you know what else, Mom? . . . Watching you."

With a look of surprise in her eyes and the sound of laughter on her lips she said, "Watching me?"

"Yes, Mom, watching you," I said. "I've watched you over the years getting knocked down time and time again. But no matter how hard the blow, you always got right back up and kept on keeping on." I went on to ask her, "How many people do you know who have survived lung cancer and a brain tumor, and then went right back to work and got promoted on their job? The only thing that slowed you down were the strokes. And I know I've watched you bounce back from at least six of those. Yes, ma'am, you are my inspiration."

"Son, I love you," she said, as she put down a spoonful of grits. "I know I haven't always been the best mother I could have been."

I grabbed her hand and said, "What are you talking about? You are a great mother."

Tears started rolling down her face as she said, "I never should have left you at home alone that weekend I went to Memphis to be with Herman. Son, I'm so sorry for that."

I got up out of my chair, kneeled at her side and hugged her tight, saying, "Mama, please stop beating yourself up for that. I know you never meant to hurt me. Even then I knew you were hoping it would ultimately lead to a better life for us.

Mom, we don't have to carry our sins past Calvary. God has forgiven us. Now we have to learn to forgive ourselves."

With tears streaming she said, "All I've ever wanted is the best for you, son." I kissed her cheeks, got up off the floor and got back in my chair saying, "I know, Mom. I only want the best for you too."

I made sure she took all eight of her medicines, and I took mine. We both kept our meds in big pill boxes that separated the days of the week. That was the only way we could keep up with the schedules and doses. After breakfast, Mom would do some exercises she had learned in therapy over the years. Holding the back of the dining-room chair she began doing her squats and lunges, saying, "See, son, you don't believe me when I tell you I do my exercises. Baby, I do my exercises every day."

All I could say was "OK, Ms. Sassy."

The truth of the matter is that my mom was a winner. Just about every time she had gone into the hospital, the doctors said she wouldn't make it, but time and time again she beat all odds. Everyone always marveled at how Mom's mind stayed strong and how she maintained her sense of humor even after her body was attacked by cancer and strokes. But now she was not bouncing back as quickly. It was obvious that the strokes and COPD were starting to wear her down. But I never once heard her complain or ask "Why me?"

Even though I had AIDS, watching my mom gave me hope that even I could beat the odds. After all, I was made from the same DNA of this seemingly indestructible woman. In the 10 years that I took care of my mother not a day went by that I didn't hear her praising and worshiping God.

"Lord, I worship you for just being you," she'd say.

As I cleaned up the kitchen Mom continued her exercise routine to strengthen her legs.

"Right leg up, right leg down."

"Left leg up, left leg down."

Now that I had finished school, I dedicated more time to church and attempting to rekindle my relationship with Isaac. We got back into our Friday night routine of dinner and a movie.

But for the next year job searching became my main focus. Every day I was surfing the Internet in hopes of finding an entry-level television reporter position. I was sending résumés, cover letters and demo tapes to stations in Birmingham, but I was also looking in medium-to-small-size markets all over the Southeast. Then it hit me. *What if I get a job in another city? Would Mom be willing to move with me, and could I take care of her if she did?* I couldn't just leave my mom at home alone. I had to talk to her.

"Mom, I need to ask you a serious question. If I get a job out of town, are you going to go stay with Aunt Jean?"

With a serious tone she asked, "Stay with Jean? Nawl, I'm going to stay right here in my house. I can take care of myself."

"Mom, you cannot stay by yourself," I said.

"I think you're exaggerating now," she said. "I've only fallen a few times. But I'm better now, 'cause I'm doing my exercises."

With my own stern voice I repeated, "Mom, you *cannot* stay by yourself." Then I asked her, "If I can't find a job here in Birmingham, would you be willing to move out of town with me?"

"Sure, I'd love to get out of Birmingham," she said with a smile.

But I added, "If I'm working out of town I may not be able to come home and check on you every day."

She paused for a second and said, "Son, we'll make it just fine."

The mood changed when I said, "Mom, you know we have

always said the day could come when either one of us could end up in a nursing home. Are you still open to that?" My heart started beating fast as I waited for an answer.

"No, I don't want to go to a nursing home," she said.

Even though we had discussed it time and time again, a nursing home was looking more like a real necessity nowadays.

Mom had nurses coming in a few days a week to help her. But I was the one responsible for her overall well-being. It's a responsibility that I not only took seriously, but I welcomed. There is an old phrase that says love is in the details. That's the way I approached the care I gave my mother. Not only did I make sure she was clean even under her fingernails, I also made sure she maintained her sense of style.

Because of the weakness in her body, it took her awhile to get dressed. But when she did she'd always call me to her room to help with the finishing touches. Then standing in front of the full-length mirror she'd flash that smile and do her shimmy.

I'd drive my mother wherever she wanted to go. That included the doctor, therapy, church, and out to eat with Aunt Jean. Mom loved her family dearly. That's why it would be hard to uproot her and move to another city.

But after about a year of job searching and denial letters, I had decided that maybe becoming a reporter was not what God was calling me to be. Maybe he had changed the plan for my life. In fact, I had decided to just give up on the idea. Then in his own unique way, God whispered in my ear.

"Go back to your computer one more time."

So I did, and ended up on a job website that I don't even remember keying in. That's where I saw a position available for an arts reporter at Mississippi Public Broadcasting in Jackson, Mississippi. Even though I didn't have the experience that the job required, something told me to apply anyway. About a month later I received an e-mail from a producer at MPB. He acknowledged that they had received my résumé and demo tape and wanted me to come over for an interview.

I jumped up from the computer and ran into the living room yelling, "Yahoo! Mom, guess what?!"

"What, son?"

"I have a job interview."

"Great! Who is it with?"

"It's with Mississippi Public Broadcasting in Jackson. They're looking for an arts reporter."

Mom stood up from the table and opened her arms up to hug me. "Son, I am so happy for you. I know you'll do well in the interview."

My interview was scheduled for nine o'clock on a Monday morning. But before I left I made sure Mom had taken her medicines and had everything she needed.

"Mama, I've already fixed your breakfast. All you have to do is pop it in the microwave. Mrs. Bell and Aunt Jean are going to be checking on you."

Mrs. Bell was our next-door neighbor. She and her husband had looked after me and my mom for years. They didn't have any kids, so I took it upon myself to adopt them as my grandparents.

By the time I was leaving, Mom had slowly made her way up to the living room.

"Mama, you didn't have to get up."

"I had to come see you off. I know you're gonna do well."

"Thanks, Mama. I'll be checking on you."

"Son, you be careful," she said as I opened the door.

Birmingham to Jackson takes a little over three and a half hours. I spent the first 20 minutes listening to Tom Joyner's

Morning Show. But this particular morning I just wanted to commune with God. I just wanted to worship him. The car was suddenly filled with the sound of my voice in praise.

"Lord, you are awesome!"

"You're magnificent!"

"There is no one else like you, Lord."

"I worship you, Lord."

I continued in the spirit of worship all the way to Mississippi.

When I got to the state line, I did my crossing ritual of blowing the horn, and as I crossed over, the sun seemed to shine a little brighter. The trees seemed a little greener, and the world around me seemed to be a little bit calmer. I didn't feel any stress or even any anxiety about the interview. My mind was in perfect peace.

I arrived in Jackson around morning rush hour, and I remember being surprised and saying to myself, "Oh, this is not too country." In Alabama, we always thought Mississippi was a little more rural than we were. When I got near downtown Jackson, I was quickly into bumper-to-bumper traffic. To my left was what I thought could have been downtown, but there didn't seem to be a defined skyline. After seeing the capitol dome I concluded that it was the heart of the city.

I arrived at the MPB complex about 15 minutes early. The lobby was filled with glistening plaques and trophies that the television and radio divisions had won over the years. Just before 9 a.m. I was whisked into the main boardroom. Nearly half-a-dozen people were waiting around a table that was so large it nearly filled the room. I remember being directed to the head of the table. With what I hoped would be an icebreaker for everyone, I jokingly said, "Aha, the hot seat." Someone laughed and said, "All right, you gotta come on with it now."

There didn't seem to be any tension in the room. We all

just talked about Birmingham and other parts of Alabama. They wanted to know about my knowledge of Mississippi. They also wanted to get an understanding of my appreciation for the arts. Finally, the director of Human Resources asked a question that turned the focus of the interview.

"What are your long-term goals?"

My response was, "I hope to eventually become a news anchor." At that moment he lit up and said, "You have to meet Teresa. She's our News and Public Affairs director. As a matter of fact, there is a position I think you would be perfect for."

After the interview I was introduced to Teresa. It was a pleasant surprise that Mississippi, a state known for its racist past, would have a black woman directing news programming on its statewide radio station. We talked briefly, and she gave me a quick tour of the facility. Even though I thought I had done well, MPB had also made a good impression on me.

On the way back to Birmingham I was riding on cloud nine. I called to check on Mom and give her my impression of how things went. The rest of the trip I was thanking God and calling Lois, TJ, Isaac and Gwen to tell them all the details. I got back to Birmingham shortly before five that evening. As I was placing my foot on the last step leading to my front porch my cell phone rang. I went inside and motioned for Mom not to say anything.

The voice on the other end said, "Hello, may I please speak with Lawayne?"

"This is he."

"Lawayne, this is Teresa Collier, news director with MPB. I just had a chance to read your résumé and view your demo tape and I like it."

"Really?" I said. "Well, thank you very much."

With a hint of laughter in her voice she said, "I know you

just left, and I'd hate to ask you to turn around . . ." I chuckled as she continued, "but we would love to have you come back so we can talk more. What we have available is a local host position for *Morning Edition*. It's a bigger job than you applied for, but we think you may be able to do it. Would you be available to come back down maybe 1 day next week?"

I said, "Sure."

"Great!" She said, "I'll be in touch, and it was nice meeting you."

As soon as I hung up the phone I hollered out, "That was MPB asking me about coming back down to interview for a job hosting *Morning Edition*."

Mom and I talked about my visit and interview in Mississippi the rest of the night.

The next week I returned to Jackson, but this time the number of people sitting in on the interview had increased and the questions were tougher. And because of my inexperience, I flubbed on the simplest questions.

"What are the call letters of the public radio station in Birmingham?"

"What newspapers do you read daily?"

"What are you favorite NPR programs?"

By the time the interview was over I felt like I needed to be wrung out and hung up on a line to dry. I didn't hear from MPB for several weeks. Even though I didn't think my chances of getting the job there were great, it didn't dampen my spirit. Now I was more encouraged than ever so I continued sending out demo tapes and résumés.

That Sunday while lying across the bed I received a phone call from TJ.

"Are you watching the Tom Brokaw special on Jackson? It's on now." He said, "Turn to Channel 13."

Tom Brokaw was doing a documentary called *Separate and Unequal: 40 years after the civil rights movement.* He was taking an in-depth look at the progress that's been made in Jackson and the problems that persist.

The show pointed out a number of changes in the city, including its black leadership. But it also painted Jackson as a city laden with crime, poverty and few opportunities for minorities, especially black youth.

After watching the special I was even more hopeful that I would get the job. My reasoning was so that I could serve as a role model and offer inspiration for the city's young people. Besides, being in Jackson would be considered an honor since most young reporters have to start out in small towns like Greenville, Mississippi, or Andalusia, Alabama.

Isaac and I had been looking forward to getting a new start away from Birmingham. As the weeks passed, I continued sitting at the computer looking for places to send my résumé. Then one day that still small voice spoke to me again.

"E-mail Teresa and thank her again for the opportunity to interview with them."

I obeyed the spirit and sent the e-mail right away. Five minutes later, Teresa was calling. She told me the position I interviewed for had been filled. However, she said there was an entry-level reporter position that she felt I would be perfect for.

That little voice did it again.

I got the job.

EIGHTEEN

JUST LIKE HE SAID HE WOULD

"OH, TASTE AND see that the Lord is good; Blessed is the man who trusts in Him!" Psalm 34:8.

I've trusted the Lord's goodness many times over. Still, I knew leaving Birmingham was one of the most bittersweet decisions I'd ever make. Yes, I had confidence that God would never leave me or forsake me. I am also a witness that if we delight ourselves in him he will direct our paths.

Even though I wanted to take Mom to Jackson with me, I knew it wouldn't be possible with the long hours I'd be working. My preference would have been for her and Aunt Jean to live together. But I also knew they were both too sickly to be much more than good company for each other. Mom needed someone to be there for her nearly around the clock. And they both needed someone to check in on them throughout the day and night.

Delois suggested her housekeeper, Clothea, a dark-skinned, short, stout, talkative woman. Clothea had taken care of her brother who had also suffered a number of strokes, but he died a few years back. Since then, she was taking care of an elderly blind man. But a week before I got the job at MPB, his daughter began taking care of him. Once again, God seemed to be moving everything into position.

Mom was so happy that I had the job in Jackson, and even though she didn't like it, she knew she needed someone to live with her.

I remembered Clothea from church and my cousin's house sometimes when I would visit. However, we had never had any real dealings with each other. A few days before I was to leave for Jackson, I brought Clothea over to meet my mother and our dog Tyson, a black lab-chow mix. Although Tyson looked ferocious, he was as gentle as a lamb.

When I picked Clothea up, the first thing she said was, "Oh, Mr. Wayne, it's so good to see you. Thank you so much for this opportunity to take care of Miss Childrey. I promise you I'm gonna take good care of your mother."

"Wait a minute, wait a minute, wait a minute," I said laughing. "Clothea, I really appreciate you being here for us, but let's get one thing clear." Then I paused, "You don't have to call me Mr. Wayne." She was fine with that and with the news that we had a dog.

As we pulled into the driveway Clothea said, "Oh, y'all live over here by Tricia Ann 'nem."

"Yeah, I forgot you know Tricia Ann from church."

"Yeah, I know Tricia Ann, Samantha, all of 'em."

When we got into the house, Tyson greeted us at the door sniffing Clothea and wagging his tail. Stooping down to pet him she said, "Hey, there Tyson, man. Ooh, he so friendly. He's a good li'l dog."

Mom was sitting back in her wheelchair watching with a smile and said, "You must be Clothea?"

"Yes, ma'am, Miss Childrey, I'm Clothea."

"Well, it's nice meeting you, Clothea."

"Miss Childrey, Miss Childrey, Miss Childrey, it's so good seeing you again. You don't remember me from the church and over Miss Delois's house?"

Mom said, "Oh, yes, I do. I just didn't recognize you with that hairstyle."

"And ooooh, Miss Childrey, I love these cornrows. Who did these for you?"

"A friend of my son."

"Well, honey, she did a great job, but you've always had pretty hair anyway. And, honey, I love that yellow jogging suit. That's silk, ain't it? And those tennis shoes are so white. Miss Childrey, you always have dressed nice. You're such a pretty woman, too."

Finally Mom was able to get a word in. "Thanks, Clothea, you're looking good yourself, girl."

"Thank you, Miss Childrey, honey. I try to always do something to keep my spirits up," she answered.

I said, "Clothea, let me show you around . . . Of course, this is the kitchen."

Clothea called across the room saying, "Oooh, Miss Childrey, I hope you like some collard greens, black-eyed peas, candied yams, corn bread and all that good stuff."

I said, "Lord, yes! Clothea, she can eat now."

"Good, Miss Childrey, I'm gone fix us some quiche, Caesar salad, baked and grilled meats, all that good stuff. It ain't gone be all soul food. But we gone be cooking up something in this kitchen though."

We continued the tour with her room.

She said, "Oh my God, Wayne, this so nice. And all this closet space. Yes, Lord, this is gone be nice."

I then took Clothea to my mom's room. It was as clean as a whistle. Even though Mom had gotten to the point where she needed a bedside commode and disposable pads on the bed, the house always smelled fresh. Based on the way Clothea kept my cousin's house spotless and the way she took pride in the way she dressed I thought she'd be the perfect person for Mom.

Isaac and I drove over to Jackson the Saturday before I was to start work. We wanted to go ahead and get settled into the apartment we had found a few weeks earlier. He had promised me months before that if I found a job outside of Alabama he would move there with me. Once again, however, it was just another broken promise. He wasn't staying.

That Sunday morning we were in the laundry room folding clothes when it hit me. Not only was Isaac preparing to leave and head back to Birmingham, but everything and everyone I loved would now be hundreds of miles away.

Tears began rolling down my face and down Isaac's too. I guess we both realized that the move would eventually mean the end of our years together, including the many ups and downs.

With the new move came new challenges. Unlike all the times before, I wouldn't have the support of my family and friends to fall back on if something went wrong. I was truly on my own. That night before I went to sleep I thanked God for everything he had done for me, including allowing my childhood dream of becoming a news reporter to finally come true.

September 11th was my first day on the job at MPB. But on this 9/11, I wasn't covering terrorism. My first assignment dealt with the issues surrounding the dangers of teen drinking and driving. I'll never forget it. This was real reporting. When I drove onto the campus of Madison Central High School, I could see about three other news stations there. I introduced myself and conducted an interview with Mississippi's attorney general. Even though it was my first assignment, I didn't feel as nervous as I thought I would be as a rookie reporter. That was the beginning of hundreds of stories I'd cover. Because we were a statewide news agency, I reported stories from the Tennessee state line to the Mississippi Gulf Coast and from the Alabama border to the Mississippi River.

Many of my days were spent in the Mississippi Delta, home of the Delta Blues and famous blues legends like Muddy Waters and B. B. King. Civil rights icon Fannie Lou Hamer, who coined the phrase, "I'm sick and tired of being sick and tired," was also from there. And Emmett Till, a 14-year-old African American boy was killed in the Mississippi Delta for allegedly whistling at a white woman. Within my first year, I saw more of Mississippi than I had seen of Alabama my entire life. I spent countless hours traveling the highways and interstates covering a wide range of topics, including politics, economics, education and health.

These are a few of the headlines I've covered over the years:

Black and White Teens from D.C. Take Bus Tour to Explore Race Relations in Mississippi

USDA Reports on Household Hunger in Mississippi

City Leaders from across Mississippi Rally at the State Capitol

The Gulf Coast Is Still Struggling Economically from BP Oil Spill

Mississippi Has the Third-Highest Number of Gun Deaths in the Nation

In what seemed like the twinkling of an eye I was finally living my childhood dream. In addition to reporting I was producing a daily news story, hosting *All Things Considered* and doing the daily afternoon newscasts. Things were happening so fast that I started to feel overwhelmed. I felt myself coming unglued and was literally shaking, my heart was racing and I couldn't eat. Once again, I was having anxiety attacks. I knew it wasn't good for my health so I began counseling with Dr. Dan over the phone.

In addition, I was also dealing with issues back home in Birmingham. Nearly every day I was getting phone calls from Clothea and Mom. They were constantly at odds about everything.

"Son, this woman is going through all of my things."

"Mr. Wayne, Ms. Childrey said she didn't need me taking care of her and I have to get out."

"Son, this woman is drinking and smoking and talks to me any kind of way. She has to go."

Every weekend I found myself driving home to lay my eyes on the situation, putting out fires and to give Clothea a break.

Early on, I noticed that the house was not as clean as it should be, my mother's clothes weren't matching and her hair was often in need of washing and combing. This was not the care I had envisioned for her. But even though the arrangement with Clothea was not perfect, it was all we could afford at the time. I had to come to grips with the reality of that. So

I drew strength from something Lois had said over the years.

"I have learned to thank God for things being as well as they are."

I had to realize that even though Mom's clothes may not have been coordinated the way I would have done them, they were at least clean. And, no, I never would have filled the kitchen counters with pots, pans, griddles and canned goods like Clothea had done, but I had to appreciate the fact that she was using them to keep my mother fed. However, I did say something to Clothea when I noticed cigarette burns on the living-room sofa, just a few feet from Mom's oxygen tank.

"Clothea," I said, "you cannot smoke in this house with an oxygen tank in it."

"Mr. Wayne, I'm so sorry. I promise it won't happen again."

Between the stresses of home and the stresses of work, I felt my life was in a constant state of anxiety. It was never to the point where I wanted to hurt myself or anyone else, but Dr. Dan helped by reminding me of some of the simple things that I had learned to do on my own whenever I felt anxiety setting in. He suggested I do some deep abdominal breathing or take a brisk walk, especially before I was to go live on the air. And he reminded me that whatever was bothering me couldn't hurt me, saying, "Remember this is not an elephant, it's only a squirrel."

Finally, I gave up the evening news and focused on reporting and producing. I continued to learn and pray as I worked my craft. Instead of traveling to Birmingham every weekend, I rooted myself in a good church home where I received peace, spiritual growth and guidance.

When award season rolled around, I even won a couple of second- and third-place Associated Press awards. But I made it my goal to take first place next year.

A few months in, Mom had another stroke. This time it was so bad she needed to be placed in a nursing home. While it was something we had tried to avoid, Mom and I both realized that it really came down to a matter of safety. In a nursing home she would have constant supervision, and I would have peace of mind knowing that she had around-the-clock care.

My prayer was that God would help me find a home where the caregivers would give her the detailed attention they would give their own mother. What she got was a complete staff of attentive nurses and a great roommate who helped her maintain a good quality of life.

Things were starting to turn around for me. I was feeling better about things, and I was making fewer calls to Dr. Dan. At last I had found my groove. The next year was mine. I took first- and second-place awards at the AP ceremony, plus I won a Regional Edward R. Murrow Award for Excellence in Journalism.

I also began dating Ray, a tall, slender, light-skinned guy who worked in the health-care field. We would spend hours on the phone talking. He had me in stitches laughing at stories about his grandmother and her sense of humor. He and I were both ending relationships and found comfort in each other. But I was hesitant at first about taking things further because I didn't want to ruin our friendship. I had already had my share of loving relationships gone bad, but he helped to ease my mind about so many things. I had told Ray all of my darkest, innermost secrets, from my childhood up until my present life and he never judged me. I fell in love with his intelligence, charm, charisma, wisdom and humor. He started going home with me, and to my delight, Mom, Gwen, Lois and other family and friends gave their strong approval.

Just as my family had taken him in, his family welcomed

me. They always invited me over for family dinners and other events. His grandmother reminded me of my own grandmother, who loved to bake and give of herself to others. His mother reminded me of my own mom with her intelligence, sense of style and Southern charm. Our moms even shared the same birthday, January 14. From the day we met I knew Ray was that special someone that I could always depend on. We have always been in sync. He can complete my thoughts, and I, his. We were there for each other from the best of times to the worst. Finally, I had met my soul mate.

In the fall of 2009 I was just about to go into the news meeting when I received a phone call from the nursing home. They told me my mother had just been rushed to UAB hospital and that her condition was critical. I told Teresa what was happening, and she told me to go ahead and go now. She understood my love and deep concern.

When I arrived at the hospital, Mom was the frailest I'd ever seen. I kissed her face and sat on the side of her bed. I told her I was there, and that I loved her. Mom couldn't verbally respond because of the tube down her throat and the heavy sedation she was under. However, the single tear that rolled down her face and the look in her eyes told me that she loved me too.

When the doctors told me and Lois that Mom had developed a severe case of aspiration pneumonia and the chances of her survival were zero, it felt as if I had been hit by a freight train. The pain was deeper than anything I had felt in years, deeper than when Dr. Middlebrook told me I had AIDS, deeper than when my mother was diagnosed with lung cancer in 1986 and brain cancer a month later . . . deeper than when my aunt Von was murdered in her sleep in 1985. That pain was so acute that I seldom ever allow myself to even think about it.

But the pain of hearing my mother could die at any moment was even more excruciating.

God stepped in once again and reminded me that Mom had been through many hard trials, but her love for him never wavered. That's when I heard his still small voice saying, *"In her I am well pleased. Now it's time for her to receive her reward and rest in me."*

Years ago I would have been devastated if Mom had passed. In 1995, toward the end of my 9-month battle with crack addiction, it was me that wanted to die. That's when I talked to my therapist about the possibility of my mother's death.

He asked, "What would happen to you if your mother died?"

I remember sitting in a chair across from him almost in a daze, and my reply was, "I'd be devastated."

He said, "No, you shouldn't be devastated. Hurt? Yes. Grief stricken? Yes. But devastated? No." He said, "Nothing should ever get you to the point where you cannot go on living your life."

When Mom returned to the nursing home I took another extended leave from my job to be by her side. That whole week she was surrounded with the love of her brother, sister, other family members and close friends.

On December 9, 2009, after Aunt Jean, Uncle Sonny and other family and friends had left for the day, Lois and I stayed by Mom's side. About 11:15 p.m., Lois sat in the recliner that she had become accustomed to and asked me to play her favorite song by Kurt Carr called, "I Almost Let Go."

Within a few seconds of playing that song, my mother took her last breath as I held her in my arms.

Yes! It hurt, and I cried. But as it says in the book of Philippians, God gave me a peace beyond all understanding.

A few days after Mom's funeral I returned to work with the understanding that God would guard my heart if I kept my mind on him.

Today, I know that going back to school was not just for me. It was also to make my mother proud. I wanted her to know that I could be something special, just like she kept saying. I also know that by placing me at Mississippi Public Broadcasting, God was preparing me for the opportunity to tell of his greatness. Again, I continued to learn and pray as I worked my craft with the help of my editors, Patty and Teresa, who pushed me to do the best stories possible. In 2010, when the AP Awards rolled around, I took top honors in three events. Plus, I won two Regional Edward R. Murrow Awards and a National Murrow.

Winning a National Murrow Award is the equivalent of winning an Oscar or an Emmy in my field. Only the crème de la crème receive the award of excellence. To know that my work has been placed on par with that of journalists like Diane Sawyer, Ted Koppel and Walter Cronkite still gives me goose bumps.

The headlines in newspapers, blogs and other publications read like a dream that I'd had so many years before:

Lawayne Childrey Wins National Murrow Award

The prestigious honor was for a story I wrote and produced about a military-style program helping Mississippi dropouts get their GED.

It read in part:

"Each year more than 14 thousand students quit school before receiving their high school diploma. In Part three of our dropout awareness series MPB's Lawayne Childrey takes us to the Mississippi Youth Challenge Academy . . . a military style program where students who have already dropped out get a second chance to graduate."

With Ray, Gwen and my cousin Shinita (Aunt Jean's daughter) by my side, I flew to New York City for the formal awards banquet. Ray and Shinita wanted to attend the star-studded gala and the nearly five hundred dollar per plate dinner. As they watched from the wings they could still see my face light up as CBS News Anchor Harry Smith handed me my award in front of an audience of top national news anchors, producers and celebrities.

Amid the glitz and glamour one may expect to see at the Golden Globe or Academy Awards, I quietly began to reflect on God's goodness. In doing so, I couldn't help but think back to all the pain and challenges of life and love I'd endured. And to all the strength I'd gained from God, family, mentors and friends. Wow . . . My dreams had really come true. I know Mom was looking down from heaven with a smile on her face saying, "Son, I'm so proud of you."

As I look back on this journey, I am amazed at how God has given me respect, credibility and honor that I so often felt I couldn't achieve or didn't deserve.

Praise be to God for restoring my failing health and allowing me to excel in my career. Yet that still small voice continues to tell me there are even better days ahead. And, yes, I'll continue believing every word he says.

Now I spend much of my time mentoring students, encouraging them to follow their true passions in life and never let go of their dreams. I offer the same message of hope to those who are suffering from addiction, abuse or any situation that leaves them feeling downtrodden and in despair. The truth is, we will all have trying times in life.

Lord knows I've had my share of heartache and pain. There were many bumps in the road for me, and even though I have fallen many times, I never lost hope that God would help me to get back up. The important thing is that I learned from my mistakes and didn't allow myself to continually wallow in my sorrows. I thank God for this journey because everything that I have gone through in life has helped prepare me for what I eventually became in life. Today, I am considered by many as a successful news journalist. It's a dream that I had since I was in the third grade. But success wasn't handed to me. I had to struggle through a deep sea of adversity to achieve it.

As I look back over my life, I realize that everything I've done, every routine, every risk, every failure and every success helped to mold me into the God-fearing man I am today. Even though I have perhaps endured more challenges than most, I was determined to rise above my adversities, for I am a firm believer that to be aware is to survive. For that reason, I have learned not to let the pressures of life and love stand in the way of me pursuing my true happiness.

That still small voice continues to tug at my heart. Every day it tells me to believe in my own potential, to never give up, and most of all, to continue to believe and trust in God. I will always obey that voice. Because as it says in Philippians 4:13, "I can do all things through Christ which strengthens me." Moreover, as I continue to travel this oftentimes bumpy road of life, Proverbs 3:6 will continue to be my personal GPS: "In all thy ways acknowledge him and he shall direct thy paths."

I believe that with every fiber of my being because I know in my heart of hearts if I continue to serve him, worship, praise and adore him, he'll continue to take me beyond places I could ever imagine.

Aunt Jean

*Gwen at the
Murrow Awards*

*Jefferson State
Speech Team
at Phi Rho Pi
National Forensic
Tournament in
California.*

*Jeffeson State Community
College Speech Team
at Berry College*

Me and Mom

*Me in the mix of a Press Gaggle
with former Mississippi Gov.
Haley Barbour*

Me delivering the Keynote Speech at the MS, LA and AL HIV/AIDS Summit

Candied Interview with Civil Rights Icon Bob Moses

*Celebrating my
2010 Edward R.
Murrow win with
MPB News director,
Teresa Collier.*

*Me with Ray at
the Grand Cayon*

Celebrating graduation day with my mentor and advisor, Ray Edwards

Mom's 50th Birthday Party

My cousin Cheryl

My cousin Lois

Mentors
Dr. Janice
Ralya, and
Christine
Goss along
with
Chris and
myself

The Family
at Mom's 50th

ACKNOWLEDGEMENTS

This book would not have been possible without the support of family, friends and mentors from all aspects of life, and for all of them, I am eternally grateful.

However, there is no way this book could have ever been written without the amazing grace and mercy of God, the creator and ruler of all things. To him I give all praise, all honor and all glory.

God anointed me years ago to write this book. However, it wasn't until now that he appointed me to do so with the help of many amazing people. To Gwendolyn Hagler, my friend, confidante and mentor, thanks for believing in me when I didn't even believe in myself. To Dr. Janice Ralya, director of Forensic Speech Communications at Jefferson State Community College, I'll never forget the day you called me up and said, "Lawayne, people really need to hear your story." Janice, I also greatly appreciate your willingness to write the forward to this book. To Dr. Ray Edwards, former director of journalism at Jefferson State Community College, without your support I never would have made it out of the gate as a journalist. I offer a special thank you to Teresa Collier, news director at Mississippi Public Broadcasting, for taking a chance and giving me my first break into this crazy world of news that we live, breathe and love. Most importantly, I'd like to thank Patricia Davis (Patty) for not only her editing expertise in the news room but also for the tireless editing efforts she made to see this book become a reality. Patty, thank you for the tough critiques that helped me dig deep into the truth even when it sometimes hurt. And a very special thanks to the Alabama Community College System for posting the book's introduction on their social media sites as part of an essay contest months before it was ever published.

However, even with all of the expertise that went into the making of this book, I owe an even deeper appreciation and gratitude to all of my family. That includes each and every Childrey, Henley, Woods, Green, Pittman, Wingard, Bodiford, Pinkney, Dabney, Willis and Johnson. Thank you all for loving me unconditionally. But please know, I'll always love you more.

I am grateful for every doctor, therapist, teacher and religious leader who helped me through some of the most difficult times in my life. You said everything would be OK, and today, all is well. That includes you, Apostle Maxine Evans Gray, Reverend Joe May, Reverend J. R. Finney, Elder James Capers, Bishop O. L. Meadows and the late Elder James Henderson. In addition, I owe a debt of gratitude to all of my fellow writers and journalists for helping me to stay humbled.

Finally, from the bottom of my heart, I expressly thank my life partner, W. Ray Willis Jr. and all of my close personal friends for understanding my long nights and early mornings at the computer.

To God be the glory for all he has done.

RESOURCE GUIDE

CONTACT the CRISIS LINE
601-713-HELP(4357)
contactthecrisisline.org
For online emotional chat support visit:
Imncrisis.org

The Mission

CONTACT the Crisis Line is an interfaith telephone ministry to troubled callers. The ministry's hallmarks are the nonjudgmentalism, respect, compassion, its trained volunteers show callers; along with confidentiality, anonymity, and availability at no charge twenty-four hours a day, every day of the year.

CONTACT the Crisis Line serves all callers without regard to residence, race, color, age, gender, religion, beliefs, faith, values, sexual orientation, national origin, physical or emotional handicap, or any such category or condition.

CONTACT the Crisis Line is a fully-accredited affiliate of CONTACT USA and of Lifeline International, and is a member in good standing of the American Association of Suicidology. CONTACT the Crisis Line is not affiliated with any one religious body, but works to extend their ministries.

CONTACT the Crisis Line's mission is:

- to listen
- to counsel
- to make referrals
- to provide information
- to pray and share scriptures (if requested)
- to intervene in emergencies
- to operate a CONTACT Reassurance program
- to participate in online emotional support
- to educate volunteers for Crisis Line work and/or to be better prepared in other vital social service fields
- to extend the services of other agencies

NOTES

NOTES

CPSIA information can be obtained at www.ICGtesting.com
Printed in the USA
LVOW08s1452030515

437033LV00001B/3/P